CONTENTS

CONTENTS

REPORT OF THE CHIEF MEDICAL OFFICER
FOR 1969–1970

To the Secretary of State for Education and Science.
Madam,

INTRODUCTION

This report, which covers the years 1969 and 1970, is somewhat shorter than its predecessors and a detailed commentary on the various chapters is not therefore included in the introduction, which is concerned rather with the changing patterns of work of the school health service and its future requirements.

The general standard of health of school children has improved immeasurably since the school health service was initiated over sixty years ago. Further improvements cannot be identified readily year by year by any single objective test but such indices as we have suggest that progress continues. The main general preoccupation of the service remains that of detecting handicaps which may affect adversely the child's ability to benefit from education. Against such a background the concern of the school health service must also be to identify departures from a generally favourable trend and to suggest ways in which they can be remedied or reduced. There are areas of concern such as the increase in the numbers of pregnancies and the rising incidence of gonorrhoea in girls under the age of 16; the increases in scabies, pediculosis and ringworm; the problem of appraisal of nutrition after the changes effected in the provision of school milk and meals. Some of these problems have medical solutions while some are the consequence of changes in behaviour which have no medical solution, as for instance the undoubted increase in sexual relationships among young people. Such findings should be seen against the generally favourable background as incentives to better use of the health resources at our disposal.

There can be no doubt that a school health service is needed for the future and it would be a valuable contribution to the organisation of both health and education services to define its needs and opportunities more precisely.

Chapter II is an essay on medical examination and surveillance of school children prepared by Dr. Whitmore. It examines the changes in the methods used by the school health service in recent years, outlines some of the indices we have of children's health requirements and suggests some ways in which the school health service of the future could meet these requirements. This essay is a useful basis for discussion now rather than an attempt to lay down a future plan. The subject is one which should be examined in the context of both the preventive work done for children at all ages and the activities of hospital paediatric departments and the family doctors. It poses important questions for the future without purporting to give final answers to them.

This report is the work of my colleagues led by Dr. Esther Simpson and I record my thanks to them for their help throughout the period it covers. It has

1

been a period of closer working with colleagues in the Department of Health and Social Security with mutual benefit. In sadness I must recall the premature and sudden death in September 1970 of Dr. Brian Didsbury, who for less than a year held the co-ordinating post in which Dr. Simpson succeeded him.

I am, Madam,

Your obedient servant,

G. E. Godber.

2

CHAPTER I

THE RÔLE OF THE
SCHOOL HEALTH SERVICE

The Education Act, 1944, Section 48, places on local education authorities a duty to make arrangements for the compulsory medical inspection of school pupils and for comprehensive free medical treatment either under that Act or otherwise. Within two years of the passing of the Education Act the National Health Service Act, 1946, was passed and, since 1948, free medical treatment has been available for all children. This created a new situation which has influenced the subsequent development of the school health service. The need for separate arrangements for treatment, either medical or dental, has declined and increasing use is being made of the facilities of the National Health Service for diagnosis, assessment and treatment.

The rôle of the school health service has changed with the changing pattern of medical care and with the concurrent improvement in the health of children generally. The change has been gradual and not always appreciated by the service's critics, some of whom are still convinced that it is archaic and an anachronism. Certainly the requirements are vastly different from those of fifty or even twenty-five years ago but there are explicit functions which are just as necessary now as in 1945 or 1920.

It should be remembered, however, that for the first 40 years of its existence the school health service performed the functions of a mass medical screening programme for school children, and this before screening became a fashionable word; it was sometimes a partial substitute for a family doctor in the days before the National Health Service and it developed specialised clinical services for children at school designed to remove or alleviate impediments to education. The mere fact that some of these services became available free in 1948 did not obviate the need for the school health service to see they were invoked when necessary and to follow up afterwards.

The whole concept of detection of disease and disturbance of function at an earlier stage and younger age has developed steadily and now, rightly, includes the recognition of emotional and behaviour problems and of mental as well as physical disease. This means that the number of children entering school with unrecognised significant illness or defect is decreasing. Nevertheless, there are such children, usually those who have had little support from their family or those who have developed some medical condition in the pre-school years. In this connection it should be remembered that attendance at child health clinics, whether run by the family doctor or by the local authority, is relatively rare after the age of 2 years and that children may only be seen episodically by the family doctor in states of acute or sub-acute illness when other unrelated medical conditions are not likely to be sought nor developmental status likely to be assessed.

In an ideal situation, doctors who see children in their pre-school years would have in mind an examination not only to exclude disease but to check on the

3

progress of normal development at different ages. Apart from this kind of assessment requiring different skills, it calls for a different orientation from those acquired by doctors in the usual basic medical training, which has seldom contained a substantial preventive and social element. Some additional training is therefore required both to give competence to do this kind of work with full understanding and to enable doctors to recognise the limits of their own resources and know when to refer problems to someone else, possibly outside the medical profession, for further assessment. Medical training is directed towards recognition of the medical needs of patients, but these have to be related in children to educational needs and methods in which the school health service has an essential bridging rôle.

In infancy there is a well recognised need for screening for handicaps and for supervision of development in the absence of definable illness. There is planned prophylaxis of communicable disease and an increasing amount of attendance at child health centres and at the clinics some family doctors hold, but attendance at the clinics and the request for advice from the family doctor are least likely to come from those families most in need of help. It is with this section of the population that so much depends on the work of health visitors, social workers and others who visit individual homes, giving advice and persuading parents when it is necessary to seek help from doctors. This also is the group which will require subsequent care from the school health service as well as preparation to secure the best placement in school. Assessment centres are being established by some hospitals with local health department participation, but assessment of handicap in a child must be a continuing process moving on into the educational field as school entry approaches.

It is likely, therefore, that a large proportion of children who have problems are well known and documented before they go to school. With the increase in interest in developmental medicine it is hoped that this proportion will steadily increase so that in time the medical examination of school entrants should be seen as a stage in a process of continuing assessment rather than, as at present, a mean of establishing a base-line. Up to now, although much should be known about the handicaps of some children, the examination of school entrants has been carried out as if there had been no pre-school assessment; and indeed there has been no such assessment for most children, at least not with their educational requirements in view. The future objective should be the reassessment of children who have already had their major medical problems identified; such reassessment taking place in a learning situation and in a group larger than the child has previously experienced. Implications of problems in a school situation may be very different from those at home and other problems may not come to light until after a child has started school.

At present, however, it seems to be necessary to retain a medical review of children when they go to school, particularly for those whose parents have not taken them to child health centres in the pre-school years, or to the family doctor except for specific treatment or prophylaxis. Assessment of how a child is responding to school life has implications for the timing of such an examination. It must be made after he has been in school long enough for teachers to be able to say how he is settling into the school community, if his behaviour is acceptable (remembering that mothers generally and naturally accept behaviour standards at home very different from those tolerable in a classroom), and also to see how he has responded to his introduction to education. This kind of assessment of

4

response to education is an on-going one and children will produce difficulties in adjustment and in learning at different stages in their school life. Teachers, psychologists, doctors, social workers, therapists of various kinds, as well as parents, may all be involved in this kind of assessment of a child's changing needs, and at different stages modification in the school programme may be required for some children. It is necessary to build up a detailed assessment based on the child's strengths and weaknesses, both physical and intellectual, and to use this assessment in planning a remedial programme if this is required. All children at some time or other need individual help with their problems, particularly children with learning difficulties, personality problems and physical handicaps. No child has quite the same pattern of abilities and disabilities as another so that it is quite logical that each should be dealt with on an individual basis. Of course, most children need little intervention from the school health service, but some need a great deal and that group needs a positive screening programme for its identification. In order that this sort of work should be most successful the school doctor, in addition to being specially trained and well able to work closely with family doctors, paediatricians and child psychiatrists, has to establish a good relationship with both head teachers and class teachers, as well as with psychologists and others concerned with a child's education. This cannot be done unless the school doctor is able to visit the same schools frequently and has both opportunity and time to talk to teachers. There must also be an established source of medical advice for the local education authority itself and this must be a doctor with special experience of the educational problems of the handicapped. The responsibility for recognising and reporting on children who are not making satisfactory educational progress or who, in school or at home, show emotional or behaviour instability, or any evidence of ill health, is shared by a number of people. This sharing of responsibility helps to bring parents, teachers and doctors closer together, focusing their attention on those children most in need of medical advice and help.

Knowledge of the administrative side of the education service is also an important factor. This combination of educational, medical and administrative information should put the school doctor in a very strong position when it comes to helping and advising parents, teachers and administrators about individual children, and should also be of particular benefit in their liaison duties with other doctors who are concerned with the more purely medical aspects of child health.

Clinical care of sick children rests with family doctors and hospital specialists —mainly paediatricians. Both family doctors and paediatricians are beginning to concern themselves more with developmental paediatrics and the work of child health centres and the school health service, but they need the third member —the doctor, whose experience lies in translating the results of precise clinical appraisal into the reasons for an adjustment of the educational programme to the needs of the individual child so far as that is practicable. Social paediatrics—the name that is sometimes given to this work—is like most of social medicine an exercise in appraisal of community needs and the effectiveness of the services provided to meet them. Dr. R. B. Hunter's working party on the work of the community physician will provide the medico-administrative background into which this group of doctors will fit, but they will be a specialised group with a major continuing responsibility in which both education and medicine have a part.

5

Staff of the School Health Service

Although there was some uncertainty about the future organisation of health services in England and Wales during 1969/1970 and principal school medical officers in some areas found that this made recruitment of staff difficult, the number of doctors working in the school health service increased during 1969 as compared with 1967. The increase was in terms both of full-time and part-time service. For the first time the statistics in Table I of Appendix B differentiate between general practitioners working part-time in the school health service and other doctors doing so, so that direct comparisons cannot be made with the findings in previous years. However, the total of all doctors working part-time in school health work increased from a full-time equivalent of 152 in 1967 to a full-time equivalent of 183 in 1969. Medical officers working full-time in local authority service also increased so that the equivalent of whole-time available to the school health service rose from 779 in 1967 to 798 in 1969. The number of individual doctors involved in providing general school health services rose from 2,914 to 3,204. However, the proportionate increase in school population was marginally greater. The number of nurses, speech therapists, physiotherapists and other ancillary workers also showed an increase.

School Population

In the period under review, the maintained school population rose from 7,080,332 (England) and 460,392 (Wales) to 7,404,309 (England) and 479,595 (Wales). Concurrently, the number of children inspected by school doctors fell slightly from 3,075,780 to 2,856,962 in English schools, and from 158,539 to 154,552 in Welsh schools. This fall was to be expected as more authorities adopted the selective system of medical examinations and it was the subject of comment in the annual reports of many principal school medical officers.

As in previous years, the large majority of children seen were healthy but there are still a large number of entrants to school who have handicaps, actual or potential, some of them previously undetected. Reference is made elsewhere in the report to the timing of medical examination of children starting school.

Research

School Child Chest Survey

This survey, carried out by Professor D. D. Reid and his colleagues, in collaboration with a number of principal school medical officers, was completed in 1969 and was reported in full in 1970.[1] Professor Reid has shown in an earlier study how evidence had been accumulating that bronchitis in early adult life depended at least in part on experience of respiratory disease in early childhood and that environmental factors such as air pollution also had an important part to play in the aetiology.

In co-operation with school doctors in a number of areas in England and Wales, Professor Reid and Dr. Colley surveyed a large number of children, recording social class, signs and symptoms of respiratory disease and the local level of air pollution. The results showed a definite social class gradient in the

---

[1] Colley and Reid. Brit. Med. J. 1970. ii. 213–217.

frequency of chronic cough, history of bronchitis, and also of disease of the ears and nose. When the recorded level of local air pollution was related to the frequency of chest illness a consistently higher level was found only among children of semi-skilled and unskilled workers. The trends in childhood chest illness were similar to those relating to severe and disabling bronchitis among adults in the same area.

Nutrition Surveys

The field-work in the survey which the Department of Clinical Epidemiology and Social Medicine at St. Thomas's Hospital, under the direction of Professor Walter Holland, made in Kent with the co-operation of the Health and Welfare Department of Kent County Council and the Department of Health and Social Security, was completed in 1969. This survey included a detailed investigation of the diet, socio-economic circumstances and clinical condition of a sample of school children in Kent. Similar surveys are being planned in Newcastle, again in collaboration with the school health service, and in Birmingham.

National Child Development Study

The second follow-up of the cohort of children born in 1958 and included in the Perinatal Mortality Survey took place in 1969. Many local education authorities have a large number of children in this cohort and the additional examinations and collection of information about them involves school doctors in a good deal of additional but very interesting work. In the report of the first follow-up of these children generous acknowledgment was made of the help provided by teachers, school doctors, school nurses, health visitors and others who were involved in tracing children and subsequently interviewing, testing and examining them. It will be remembered that the long-term aims of this particular study are to gather information about educational progress, health and development, as well as about the home background, and to evaluate the effectiveness of the medical and educational provision for handicapped and for exceptional children.

These few examples of additional work accepted by school doctors are an important indication of one of the rôles of the school health service. There is considerable value in collaboration of this kind and on this scale, and research projects, many of them based in academic departments, are facilitated by the generous allocation of professional staff time by local education authorities.

Handicapped School Leavers

The Principal School Medical Officer for Cheshire reported on a survey made by a social worker, of adolescents who had left special school or had ceased home tuition before September 1967 and some other handicapped people in the 16–23 age group: it was only a small survey starting with 87 individuals, 37 of whom were excluded for various reasons (mental subnormality, handicap only temporary, moved away before survey started). Of the remaining 50, only 17 were able to get about fairly well. More than half of them had no daily occupation of any kind and having been considered unsuitable for further training there was no alternative provision and many of these young people were at home, admittedly some of them from choice as they had deliberately withdrawn from outside contacts.

Isolation was the most common problem, especially for those who had had long periods of home tuition and very little contact therefore with people their own age. Forty per cent of those interviewed were totally dependent on relatives and the strain on these relatives was very great indeed, especially when arrangements for short-term residential care to give the rest of the family some relief were not easily made. Similarly, it was difficult to arrange for the disabled member of the family to have a holiday. This relatively small but interesting and illuminating survey underlines the responsibility that education authorities have towards the children in their care to ensure, as far as possible, that those responsible for organising services for them after they leave school are made aware in good time of the special needs of these young people. Most families with a handicapped member carry their additional burden willingly and cheerfully to the limit of their ability but their task can be extremely onerous and it could be made much easier if more help were made available in some cases.

CHAPTER II

MEDICAL EXAMINATION AND SURVEILLANCE OF SCHOOL CHILDREN

Section 48(1) of the 1944 Education Act requires local education authorities '. . . to provide for the medical inspection, at appropriate intervals, of pupils in attendance at any school or country college maintained by them . . .'. A series of Regulations issued since the Act have stipulated in more specific terms how local education authorities should meet this duty. The Handicapped Pupils and School Health Service Regulations, 1945, required children to be examined as soon as possible after entry to school, in the last year of attendance at primary school and during the last year in secondary school. Many authorities arranged an additional examination on transfer to junior school at the age of approximately 8 years. These Regulations were replaced in 1953, by the School Health Service and Handicapped Pupils Regulations, which gave the Minister power to approve fewer than three statutory medical inspections of every pupil. Authorities were initially slow to take advantage of this freedom to modify their arrangements for medical examinations. Six years after the introduction of the new Regulations only one authority had adopted a scheme throughout the county that omitted the routine examination of every child during his last year in primary school; fourteen authorities had sought and received approval to try out limited schemes of a similar nature.

In 1959, a third revision of the Regulations was introduced. This revision (the School Health Service Regulations, 1959), which is still current, does not repeat regulation 10(1) of the 1953 Regulations, prescribing the frequency of medical inspection: neither the entrant nor leaver examination is now statutory and a minimum number of examinations during school years is not stipulated. Circular 352 (24 March 1959) accompanying the Regulations pointed out that the duty of authorities regarding medical inspection is stated sufficiently clearly in the 1944 Education Act; and whilst it advised that three examinations should take place between the ages of 5 and 14 when an authority carried out this duty by means of periodic routine inspections it commended arrangements whereby only children brought to the attention of the school doctor by parent, teacher or school nurse should be examined if the doctors were able to visit each school regularly e.g. at least two or three times each term.

By 1961, 37 local education authorities (20 county boroughs and 17 county councils) were either operating, experimenting with or about to initiate pilot studies of 'selective' arrangements that did not involve the examination of all children at three specified ages; the great majority were using a variety of methods (but principally a parental questionnaire) to select individual pupils for examination within the 10-to 12-year-old age group.

9

The Pattern of Examination in 1968

Seven years later, in 1968, 12 of these authorities had given up such arrangements but 47 other authorities had become interested in them, making 72 authorities in all (45 per cent of local education authorities) who were using them. Forty-three authorities were county boroughs and 29 were county councils but modified arrangements were proportionally more often operating in the latter.

A study of the annual reports from principal school medical officers for 1968 shows that the pattern of medical examinations is now very varied. The picture is complicated by the use by some authorities of the term 'selective' or 'special selective' for the examinations of children, either from a given age group or at any age, specially referred by parent, teacher or medical officer, whether or not there appears to the examining doctor to be any medical justification for an examination. Some authorities have been forced to accept such examinations by referral through lack of doctors to carry out either routine inspections or the more traditional kind of selective examinations; others have adopted the same arrangements as a matter of policy. A breakdown of the schemes of the 72 authorities that have modified their examination arrangements shows the following:

1 authority selects from among school entrants and thereafter examines only children specially referred by parent or teacher:

the remaining 71 authorities routinely examine all entrants but their schemes thereafter vary;

7 depend solely on special referrals throughout the school years;

6 carry out routine inspections or interviews of all school leavers and examine special referrals during the intervening years;

1 uses selective methods only for children aged about 8 years and for leavers;

4 use selective methods only for children aged about 10 to 12 years, and for leavers;

2 use selective methods only for children aged about 8 years, 10 to 12 years and for school leavers;

4 use selective methods only for 8-year-old pupils and routinely examine all leavers;

32 use selective methods only for children aged 10 to 12 years and routinely examine all leavers;

6 use selective methods only for school leavers and routinely examine all children aged 10 to 12 years;

9 use selective methods only for children aged 8 and those aged 10 to 12 years, and routinely examine all leavers.

Where selective examinations have been used, 38 authorities have applied these procedures to the whole of the age group concerned whereas in 20 authorities selective procedures have been only partially adopted, mainly because of the interest of individual school doctors who have applied them or are experimenting with them in certain schools only. In some instances these arrangements have been continued for many years. In three authorities it is left to the discretion of individual medical officers whether they routinely examine the children in their schools or select certain children only for examination.

10

From an *ad hoc* enquiry carried out in 1967, Lunn[1] reported that 54 per cent of children in the intermediate age group in 71 local education authorities using intermediate selective examinations were included in selective arrangements, and 66 per cent of school leavers were included in leaver selective arrangements being used by 22 authorities. In all, 40 per cent of the eligible children had been selected for examination.

The reports from individual authorities using selective methods in 1968 indicated a wider range in the proportion of pupils selected, from less than one per cent to 69 per cent, with a mean of about 28 per cent for all the children concerned and approximately the same mean for each of the three age groups to which selective schemes of examinations applied. Nevertheless, these selective arrangements in nearly half the local education authorities had very little impact on the national pattern of post-entry individual examinations, reducing the number of routine examinations of children in England and Wales in 1968 by only 10 per cent, compared with previous years.

The manner in which children are selected for examination varies slightly from one authority to another but the methods employed by Stockport in 1968 appear to be typical: 'Health questionnaires, accompanied by covering letters, are sent to the parents of all children in the eight and eleven year old groups. When completed, these are returned to the school medical officer in sealed envelopes marked "Confidential". As a result of scrutiny of these questionnaires the school medical officer decides which children merit examination. However, before the final list of such children is drawn up, the school medical officer consults with the head teacher in order to determine whether any significant condition, which may have escaped the notice of the parents, has been observed at school. A scrutiny of the school register indicates any excessive absenteeism and this in itself leads to the child being selected for examination, irrespective of the results of the questionnaire.'

Rather more than half the authorities in England and Wales have continued to organise periodic medical inspections of all pupils at specified periods in their school life when there is no valid evidence that this is the most effective use of limited medical personnel in meeting the needs of school children and when authorities have had plenty of opportunity to study alternative arrangements for the last 18 years. It may therefore be helpful to review the object of medical examinations of pupils and the methods of arranging them.

Defects Found at Medical Inspections

The principal defects found at periodic and special medical inspections and their prevalence per 1,000 pupils in certain age groups are set out in Table I. The figures refer to England and Wales in 1963 and 1968.

Six kinds of disorder account for 80 to 90 per cent of the defects recorded in children in each of the three age groups examined periodically. Among entrants, these disorders are: defects of eyes, of nose and throat, of ears, orthopaedic conditions, skin lesions and speech defects. Among children aged 8 to 13 years and among school leavers, the six commonest conditions are the same as among entrants (though not in the same order of frequency) except that speech defects are displaced by psychological disorders.

---

[1] Lunn, J. E. (1967). Medical Officer, 15 December.

TABLE I

Prevalence of certain defects (including visual) requiring treatment per 1,000 pupils examined at various ages
England and Wales—1963 and 1968

	Entrant examinations		Intermediate examinations		Leaver examinations		Special examinations	
	1963	1968	1963	1968	1963	1968	1963	1968
Eyes: vision	30·1	33·2	81·4	78·8	93·4	90·7	85·2	69·1
squint	16·4	14·9	9·9	9·6	4·6	3·9	12·1	7·0
other	2·7	2·3	2·9	2·4	2·3	1·9	15·9	10·1
(total)	49·2	50·4	94·2	90·8	100·3	96·5	113·2	85·2
Nose and throat	26·4	21·2	11·6	11·2	6·2	6·2	24·0	16·5
Orthopaedic: feet	14·5	11·2	12·7	10·2	7·2	6·5	10·4	8·2
posture	2·3	1·4	4·5	2·6	4·7	3·0	3·0	1·6
other	7·3	5·2	6·7	5·5	6·8	4·8	11·4	8·6
(total)	24·1	17·8	23·9	18·3	18·7	14·3	24·8	18·4
Ears: hearing	8·5	12·0	6·0	8·8	3·7	4·0	16·5	20·1
otitis media	4·2	5·0	2·4	3·2	2·3	2·0	4·9	3·8
other	2·6	2·4	2·5	2·1	2·9	1·7	12·1	10·5
(total)	15·3	19·4	10·9	14·1	8·9	7·7	33·5	34·4
Skin	10·1	12·4	14·2	18·2	19·0	21·9	106·3	96·8
Speech	8·6	9·7	4·4	4·6	1·3	1·1	9·1	8·5
Psychological	4·6	5·9	9·3	13·5	3·7	5·1	17·2	23·9
Sub-total	138·3	136·8	168·5	170·7	158·1	152·8	328·1	283·7
Neurological: epilepsy	1·0	1·1	1·3	1·7	1·0	1·3	1·4	1·5
other	1·5	1·5	1·8	2·0	1·0	1·0	2·5	2·9
(total)	2·5	2·6	3·1	3·7	2·0	2·3	3·9	4·4
Developmental: hernia	1·9	2·1	1·0	1·1	0·4	0·5	0·6	0·6
other physical	2·8	3·9	4·2	6·0	2·2	3·3	3·1	5·0
(total)	4·7	6·0	5·2	7·1	2·6	3·8	3·7	5·6
Lungs	8·1	7·4	5·0	5·9	3·0	3·5	6·5	5·3
Heart	2·5	2·5	1·8	2·0	1·9	1·6	2·0	1·9
All other	11·0	10·8	11·9	13·6	8·8	9·1	113·4	79·3
Total defects per 1,000 children examined	167·1	166·1	195·5	203·0	176·4	173·1	457·6	380·2
Number of children examined	662,089	718,258	793,280	635,782	554,846	449,027	665,614	535,652

12

The remaining 10 to 20 per cent of defects are principally disorders affecting lungs, heart and nervous system, and (included among 'all other defects' in Table I) nutritional state and genito-urinary system. The pattern of defects in 1968 was substantially the same as in 1963.

Varying Yield of Defects

The yield of defects (excluding visual) recorded at various medical examinations is shown in Table II. The yield of defects (180 per 1,000 pupils) among 33,474

TABLE II

Total yield of defects (excluding visual) requiring treatment per 1,000 pupils examined at various ages—1968

	Entrants' examinations (5–7 years)	Intermediate examinations	Leaver examinations (14–16+ years)	Special examinations (5–16+ years)
In England and Wales All LEAs, whether using routine or selective examinations ..	121	143 (8–13 years)	82	304
In 35 LEAs applying selective examinations covering all pupils at intermediate ages	136	180 (7–9 years) 180 (10–13 years)	102	470
In 6 LEAs applying selective examinations at various ages:				
Newcastle C.B. ..	120	132 (9–10 years)	105	443
Plymouth C.B. ..	169	239 (7–8 years)	114	397
Stockport C.B. ..	279	302 (8–9 years) 209 (11 years)	87	378
West Bromwich C.B. ..	23	31 (11–12 years)	19	166
Hampshire C.C. ..	112	92 (7–13 years)	30 (among unselected) 143 (among selected)	115
Northamptonshire C.C.	121	36 (10–11 years)	23	34

children aged 7 to 13 years selected for examination is more than twice as great as the yield (143 per 1,000 pupils) from the total of 635,782 children in the same age group that were examined in England and Wales very largely by routine periodic examinations. What is more striking is that among children aged 5 to 16 receiving special examinations (i.e. examination at the special request of parent, doctor, nurse, teacher or some other person) the yield was more than twice as great as among all children aged 8 to 13 examined by either routine or selective methods, and in the 35 authorities using selective methods which covered all pupils in the age group, the yield from special examinations was nearly three times greater than from selective examinations.

In the bottom half of Table II similar data is shown for some randomly selected authorities from among those using selective methods of examinations. The general trend of special examinations to reveal more defects (excluding visual) requiring treatment is again evident; the range of difference between

2

special and selective examinations is considerable, and so is the range of prevalence of defects within the age groups recorded. In fact, among the 72 local education authorities (previously referred to on page 10) who use selective methods of examination in one form or another, the range in the frequency of defects among entrants is from 3 per cent to 33 per cent, and among school leavers it is from 2 per cent to 20 per cent.

The higher yield of defects from special examinations is largely accounted for by the much greater number of skin conditions and of miscellaneous conditions not specified; impairment of hearing and defects of a psychological kind are also recorded more frequently at special examinations (Table I).

The annual returns from local education authorities do not provide separate data regarding the distribution of defects found at selective examinations. Such information is rarely provided in the annual reports of principal school medical officers or in the results of special studies published elsewhere. However, from the meagre data available, it would seem that selective examinations pick out in the main the same six kinds of defects as are found at periodic examinations at the intermediate stage and at special examinations at any age. Bacon[2] discussed two clear trends in the relative frequency of different types of defects found at periodic and selective examinations: a reduction in the number of orthopaedic disorders and an increase in psychological disturbances.

Selective Examinations Miss Certain Defects

A number of authorities have expressed their concern that selective examinations miss important defects and for this reason have been reluctant to modify their arrangements for periodic age-based examinations. This aspect of selective schemes has been studied more than others.

In a small pilot scheme covering 101 8-year-old children in the Isle of Wight[3] a very high degree of accuracy in selection was achieved; only one child was subsequently found to have a mild defect (and it did not require treatment) in the 38 pupils not selected for examinations.

Such a degree of accuracy has seldom been repeated in other published results. In a similar trial in one area of the City of Birmingham[4] the school doctor was disturbed to find that 60 pupils among 231 10- and 11-year-old children not initially selected for examination, when examined later had 72 (including 13 visual) defects requiring treatment. These were not previously known or if they were they had not been attended to by the parents. Experience in Scotland has been no different; in Edinburgh[5] a similar proportion (22 per cent) of unselected 9-year-old children were subsequently found to have defects needing treatment and in Dundee,[6] in a post-war development area, the figure was 20 per cent. In Hampshire,[7] a special survey after five years experience of selective medical examinations showed that whilst it was exceedingly rare for

[2] Bacon, L. (1961). Public Health, Vol. LXXV, No. 6.
[3] Ashley-Miller, M. (1965). Medical Officer, 26 February.
[4] Todman, R. C. F. (1966). Medical Officer, 22 April.
[5] Craik, I. F. (1966). Medical Officer, 22 April.
[6] Middlemiss, T. and Ward, J. A. (1961). Scottish Home and Health Dept., Vol. XXVI, No. 2.
[7] Bacon, L. (1967). Medical Officer, 10 March.

defects to come to light from alternative sources following selective inspections, examination of 434 school leavers at the age of 14 years revealed 33 defects which in all probability had been present but not detected at the last (selective) examination and another 13 that may perhaps have been present. In all, 100 school leavers were reported as having 127 new defects; it was considered that 28 defects were likely to have been missed if the school leavers had been interviewed rather than examined at 14 and that 41 defects might have been missed if they had been given selective examinations then as at the intermediate stage.

The Importance of the Defects which are Missed

How serious are the defects that are likely to be overlooked by selective examinations? The answer must depend upon the particular defect, the opinion of the individual doctor and especially from what standpoint the question is asked: whether it is in relation to the physical health of the child, his progress in learning in school subjects, his social adjustment or his personal development in general. Most reports on selective arrangements have not been at all explicit on this point. However, in the Hampshire survey, specific criteria of educational failure and medical disability were adopted in estimating that only 28 defects of the 127 new defects discovered in the school leavers examined were significant: these were identified as one case each of earache, slight hearing loss, poor circulation, varicose veins and migraine, and 23 orthopaedic defects. Orthopaedic defects are the third commonest defects found in school leavers in England and Wales and they accounted for one-third of the defects found in the Hampshire survey, but there is much controversy regarding the seriousness or need for treatment of these conditions. The experience of school doctors in Hampshire in finding that an orthopaedic surgeon considered only five children required treatment or observation of eighty referred to him as having an orthopaedic disorder, underlines the lack of measurable and standardised norms for many of the physical and developmental characteristics observed at school medical inspections.

The missed defects noted in other surveys have been more varied. As well as orthopaedic conditions they consisted of the following: squint and diminished visual acuity; otitis media and impaired hearing; skin diseases, some of which were communicable; obesity and other nutritional disorders; functional and organic cardiac disorders; bronchitis, and asthma and hayfever; epilepsy; genital abnormalities; isolated cases of thyroid disease, anaemia, toxoplasmosis and disorders of the urinary system; and finally, a few cases of intellectual retardation, speech defects and behaviour disturbances.

It cannot be disputed that potentially, according to the severity of the disorder, all these conditions are significant either for progress in learning at school or health and development in general. This being so, it must continue to be a matter of some concern that selective examinations are liable to overlook them.

Routine Periodic Examinations are also Unreliable

It may well be asked whether the kind of defects that are missed by selective examinations would be more likely to be discovered at routine examinations. It was reckoned that only one-third of the important defects missed at earlier selective examinations in Hampshire and detected at school leaver examinations were at all likely to have been found if age-based inspections had been carried out at the intermediate stage even if they had been present at that time. The routine examination has been shown to be an unreliable method of discovering defects;[8] and in one study[9] specifically designed to investigate the reliability of routine examinations, a careful re-examination by consultant paediatricians (under exceptionally good circumstances) of 562 secondary school children who were about to leave school revealed 308 defects, of which there was no record one year previously following routine examination at the age of 13 years; this represented more than half the total number of defects found in this group of children. It was considered unlikely that many of these defects had developed only in the twelve-month interval between routine and special examination.

In a small study in Birmingham,[10] 70 out of 191 defects known to be present in 266 pupils of various ages were not recorded by the school doctors at routine medical inspections, and 25 of these disorders were regarded as potentially serious. The children's family doctors knew of these (although there were others about which they were unaware). The need for the school doctor's examination of school entrants to be supplemented by information from general practitioners and hospitals, if no defects are to be missed, has been clearly demonstrated.[11]

Selective Examinations are not Sufficiently Discriminatory

Lunn, in a survey already referred to,[1] considered that selective examinations did not discriminate sufficiently well between children who do and those who do not have health problems, and Ward[6] found that selective examinations led to many children being examined who had no immediate medical needs. Several principal school medical officers have referred in their reports to the fact that inconsistent information from parents resulted in the unnecessary examination of their children.

However, the data given in Table II indicates that selective examinations do discriminate rather better than routine examinations. This is borne out by the findings from pilot studies carried out in two authorities. In Birmingham,[4] of 802 children selected for examination only one in five were healthy and without defects requiring attention, whilst of 108 children who were not initially selected for examination almost half were defect-free and healthy. A similar trial in Worcestershire[12] showed that selective examinations were twice as likely as routine examinations to result in some kind of action on the part of the school doctor: this followed in 33 per cent of 8-year-old children and 27 per cent of 12-year-olds, in six Kidderminster schools, who were selected for examination but in only 14 per cent and 15 per cent respectively of 8-year-old pupils in the whole county who were given routine examinations at those ages.

---

[8] Tizard, J., Rutter, M. and Whitmore, K. (1970). 'Education, Health and Behaviour'.
[9] The School Health Service Report of Study Group set up by Secretary of State for Scotland (1968). Scottish Home and Health Department.
[10] Asher, P. (1967). Medical Officer, 16 June.
[11] Grant, G. L. (1970). 10 April.
[1] Lunn, J. E. (1967). Medical Officer, 15 December.
[6] Middlemiss, T. and Ward, J. A. (1961). Scottish Home and Health Dept., Vol. XXVI, No. 2.
[4] Todman, R. C. F. (1966). Medical Officer, 22 April.
[12] Annual Report of Principal School Medical Officer, Worcestershire (1968).

The conclusion arrived at in Kidderminster was that 'where screening examinations are carried out at 5, 8, 11 and 14 years, and where close liaison exists between teaching staffs and the school health service, there is no point in continuing to carry out selective examinations'. However, from the information given, it appeared that the time factor was uppermost in the reasons for this conclusion. Apart from the extra clerical work involved, the saving of school doctors' time was negligible: two sessions were occupied in scrutinising 432 parent questionnaires and school medical records and eight sessions were required to examine the 164 children selected, at the rate of twenty children per session. If routine examination of all the 216 children concerned had been carried out, this would have occupied eleven sessions.

There seems no doubt that selective examinations are entirely practicable, even in a congested industrial area with a very mixed population as in Birmingham. Those who have tried these methods almost invariably agree that the parent questionnaire can be completed satisfactorily by the vast majority of parents. The meetings between school doctors, school nurses and teaching staff have been described in such terms as 'an unqualified success', 'enjoyable and stimulating for all and 'an efficient procedure and preferable to the routine medical inspection'. Yet only a minority have experienced no significant administrative difficulties; the greater number report a good deal of extra clerical work involved in sending out and sorting parent questionnaires (and teacher questionnaires, when these are used) and that the school medical officers have to spend too much time in selecting the children they consider should be examined. Some authorities interpret these consequences as evidence that selective examinations do not save time, are in fact time-consuming, and have consequently been disillusioned as regards their value. In Eastbourne,[13] for example, the diminishing return from 'time-consuming' selective procedures, including surveys of children taking physical education, were such that selective examinations were abandoned in 1968. Lunn[1] found from his enquiries of local education authorities that the additional work caused by selective schemes had led two authorities to stop them temporarily and he concluded that 'they were too cumbersome and time-consuming'. In the County of Lindsey,[14] in 1968, consideration was given to omitting the selective conference in the smaller schools so as to avoid the school doctor having to make two visits to one school in respect of only a small number of pupils. In a trial scheme in another county a few years ago it was appreciated that selective procedures could possible have been enhanced by preliminary conference between teachers, doctors and school nurses but this was considered to be extremely time-consuming and the experiment was undertaken, in part, 'to cut down the doctor's own time in any one school and that of the possible interference in the school curricula'.

In considering this criticism, it is necessary to draw a distinction between what may not be time-saving and what may be time-consuming. It is entirely understandable that with the widespread shortage of school doctors and the ever present need for the strictest economy in the administration of local authority services, principal school medical officers should be preoccupied with

---

[13] Annual Report of Principal School Medical Officer, Eastbourne (1968).
[1] Lunn, J. E. (1967). Medical Officer, 15 December.
[14] Annual Report of Principal School Medical Officer, County of Lindsey (1968).

saving medical time. Nevertheless, it has been repeatedly shown and stated that selective examinations do not save medical time and this is not their purpose.

The criticism that selective examinations are time-consuming needs more serious consideration. The aim behind these examinations is to re-deploy medical time, so that more of it is used in examining and attending to those pupils who have problems the school doctor may be able to deal with than is the case when all children of a given age are examined. This purpose could certainly be defeated if the methods of selecting a smaller number of children for a more rewarding examination took so long that more time was not available for each individual child selected. This result would only allow the claim that selective examinations were equally effective but no better than routine examinations in identifying the children most needing attention and hence no real justification (as the Kidderminster divisional school medical officer maintained) for changing a long-standing, well-organised and smoothly running scheme.

A closer study of annual reports does not confirm that an inordinate amount of time is spent in deciding which children should be examined; on average, one or two sessions depending on the size of the junior school are required for perusal of the parent questionnaires and discussion with head teachers and school nurse. What does become apparent is that school doctors regard these sessions as hours lost from time available for examining children and consider that a doctor's time is better spent examining children and talking to their parents. It is also clear that some principal school medical officers have found that more time is required for the actual examination of selected children than for children who are examined routinely and there is therefore a demand for more sessions from school doctors.

These findings suggest that, whether in their eagerness or their reluctance to modify the means of examinations, some local education authorities have lost sight of the ends that examinations seek to achieve and have been diverted into a sterile search for defects by ways and means which are the least demanding of medical officer time. It is a matter for regret that attention is given to ways of reducing opportunities for school doctors to discuss pupils with their teachers. It is a matter for surprise that, among some two hundred 9-year-old children, half of whom had defects of vision, hearing or speech, some disturbance of behaviour or emotional development, intellectual retardation or disorder of nutrition, there were only two regarding whom advice was given to the teacher.[5]

Periodic medical inspections were originally criticised as being a tedious and time-consuming exercise involving the examination of many hundreds of children to identify the 15 per cent with defects. They were further criticised on the score that they do not seek to differentiate between defects that are known to parents, whether or not they need treatment or are under treatment, and new disorders that may require treatment. They have furthermore been shown to be unreliable.

Selective medical examinations were introduced in an attempt to meet the criticisms of periodic examinations and to concentrate medical time and effort where these seemed most likely to be required and rewarding. They have in turn been criticised as being time-consuming (though in a different way from periodic examinations) insufficiently refined as a method of quickly discriminating between the children who are likely to need treatment and those who are not, and equally unreliable in identifying all those children who need treatment.

---

[5] Craik, I. F. (1966). Medical Officer, 22 April.

The fact is that as a method of surveillance of children once they have been fully examined on entry to school, neither periodic nor selective examinations are particularly efficient or economical. Selective examinations have certain beneficial side-effects, such as a closer working relationship between doctor and teacher and greater demands upon the doctor in elucidating problems. That more time is required for them is clear demonstration of how inadequate and ineffective many periodic examinations must be. Yet even selective examinations have failed entirely to satisfy the urgent need to deploy the best and the most that medicine can offer a school child, his teachers and his parents.

The answer does not lie in discarding all the procedures that characterise selective examinations any more than in a return to or a dogged maintenance of periodic examinations, which are even more outmoded. Rather, the answer may be found after taking a fresh look at the outstanding disorders and problems affecting the health and development of children today and at the ways in which the school health service can best contribute to their detection and management.

It is no longer sufficient—indeed it was never right—to state in general terms that the school health service should continue to be mainly interested in the prevention of disease and disability whilst curative medicine is the concern of the family doctor and hospital service. The latter are inescapably interested in and contributing to prevention, both primary and secondary, just as the school health service provides at least part of the treatment for some children, for example some with enuresis or asthma, and others needing speech therapy or psychotherapy. Nor is it enough, nowadays, merely to outline the basic functions of the service. It is necessary to specify the actual tasks it should undertake. These should be confined to those areas of health and those aspects of development in which its contribution is essential or more effective than that of the other medical services; it should act only in a supplementary rôle in respect of other matters of health. Duplication of services must be avoided but some overlap or interlocking of the health services for children is probably desirable to close the gaps between them.

What, then, are the major problems affecting the health and development of school children today?

Principal Disorders Affecting the Health, Development and
Learning of School Children

These are set out in Table III. Certain conclusions may be drawn from Table III that have a bearing on the tasks of the school health service and the value and rôle of routine medical examinations. More than half the deaths of children of school age and up to one in five of their admissions to hospital are due to accidents and malignant neoplasms. The school doctor can do little in a direct way to prevent these. Kerb drill and the teaching of swimming, for instance, do not require medical skills. The early recognition of a new growth that might ultimately prove fatal must be regarded as fortuitous and not one of the primary objectives of a school medical examination.

One-third of the deaths and 45–60 per cent of hospital admissions, depending on age, are due to a very limited number of conditions. Chief among these are respiratory infections which, with infections of the ears and asthma, account for 12 per cent of deaths in school children, but for 36 per cent of hospital admissions (33 per cent of all admissions of 5–9-year-old children in 1967 were for tonsillectomy), cardiac disorders, including congenital heart disease and rheumatic

TABLE III

Principal disorders of health and development in school children—1967/8

	Deaths (1968) Children		Illnesses [hospital admissions] (1967) Admissions*		Routine medical examinations		Special medical examinations Children	Handicapped pupils in [and awaiting] special schools Children Aged 2–19	
	Aged 5–9	Aged 10–14	Aged 5–9	Aged 10–14	Entrants Children Aged 5–7	Others Children Aged 8–14	Aged 5–16+ years	Prevalence per 1,000 pupils aged 2–19	% of total in each category
Total numbers	1,441	1,107	270,000	149,414				108,112	
% of totals due to:									
Accidents	37·0	36·2	12·9	18·5					
Malignant diseases	19·2	18·7	0·8	1·9					
(sub-total)	56·2%	54·9%	13·7%	20·4%					
Infectious diseases	3·5	2·9	4·4	4·3					
Bronchitis and pneumonia	7·1	7·0	1·8	1·1					*Delicate*
Other pulmonary diseases	1·5	1·5	3·6	3·2	4·4	2·5	1·4	1·3	8·7
Asthma	1·3	3·7	1·2	1·9					
Diabetes	0·7	1·4	0·4	1·1	*Data not available*				
Renal disease	1·5	1·8	1·6	1·9					
Acquired heart disease and rheumatic fever	1·1	2·7	0·2	0·7	1·5	1·0	0·5		
Congenital heart disease	7·3	4·5	0·6	0·6					
Spina bifida	1·2	0·7	0·1‡	0·1‡	4·4	2·8	1·5		
Other congenital anomalies	3·1	2·3	3·3	5·6					
Musculo-skeletal disorders	0·4	0·5	1·8	4·8	11·0	8·6	5·0	1·5	*Physically handicapped* 10·6
Cerebral palsy	1·3	2·0	0·1‡	0·2‡					
Epilepsy	1·5	2·1	0·5‡	0·9‡	0·6	0·8	0·4	0·1	*Epileptic* 0·8

20

Table (rotated 90°). Report on Hospital In-Patient Enquiry sample data.

Right-hand summary block (composition of ascertained handicapped children):

Category	*	‡
Deaf and partially hearing	7.2	0.9
Blind and partially sighted	3.3	0.5
Speech defective	0.3	0.03
Maladjusted	11.2	1.5
E.S.N.	57.9	7.8
	100%	
	100	

Main table:

Disorder	Deaf and partially hearing	Blind and partially sighted	Speech defective	Maladjusted	E.S.N.		[Nose and throat]
Acute upper respiratory diseases	1.0	0.4	3.5	1.5	12.6	4.5	4.4
Hypertrophy Ts and As	0.2	Nil	32.9	12.6	3.0	1.3	1.0
Inflammatory disease of ear and mastoid	0.4	0.5	5.8	3.2	3.0	1.3	1.0
Deafness	89.3%	88.9%	75.5%	64.1%	37.5%	21.5%	14.2%
	Nil	Nil	1.2	2.1	7.0	3.3	5.3
Squint	Nil	Nil	3.9	1.7	8.7	3.4	1.8
Refractive errors	Nil	Nil	Nil	Nil	20.0	46.0	18.2
Speech defect	Nil	Nil	Nil	Nil	5.7	1.4	2.8
Skin disease	2 children	1 child	1.3	2.8	7.6	10.8	26.4
Nutritional disorder	Nil	1 child	0.2	0.3	Data not available	Data not available	Data not available
Syphilis and gonorrhoea	89.4%	89.1%	82.1%	71.0%	86.5%	86.4%	68.7%
Illegitimate births and abortions	Nil	Nil	Nil	43 girls	Data not available	Data not available	Data not available
Psychiatric disorder	Nil	4 suicides, 2 children	0.3	0.6	3.4	4.8	6.4
Mental retardation	4 children				Data not available	Data not available	
Educational retardation	Nil	Nil	Nil	Nil	Data not available		
Miscellaneous	89.6%	89.6%	82.4%	71.9%	89.9%	91.2%	75.1%
	10.4	10.4	17.6	28.1	10.1	8.8	24.9
	100	100	100	100	100	100	100
	100	100	100	100	100	100	100

* Estimates based upon 10% sample [Report on Hospital In-Patient Enquiry—1067, H.M.S.O.].

‡ Estimate based on number of children aged 5–14 years with disorder specified.

fever and its sequelae, account for 7 per cent of deaths. Other congenital anomalies (including spina bifida) and cerebral palsy account for another 5 per cent. Four per cent of deaths in school children are due to epilepsy, diabetes and kidney disease.

Routine medical examinations identify this second group of disorders to a limited extent only, and this diminishes as the age group examined gets older. Respiratory diseases and disease of the ears are second only to errors of refraction in their frequency among defects in school entrants and it is not surprising that they are found less often in school leavers. Whilst it is well worth while spending a little time considering the child's state of resistance to respiratory infections if he is to be comprehensively examined at the age of five, arbitrarily timed intermittent routine medical inspections are not a logical method of subsequently identifying respiratory conditions in older school children. If they are significant they will reveal themselves in ways which do not wait upon routine examinations, such as through repeated or serious illness leading to absence from school (for which the family doctor is usually called for treatment, but about which the school doctor can enquire for surveillance) or impairment of function, either in a general sense as shown by lack of vitality or restriction on activities in school, or in a more specific manner, such as by impairment of hearing. A better use of the school doctor's time in reducing mortality and morbidity from respiratory disease is in health education, although it is a matter of opinion how opportune and effective a situation the routine medical examination is for health education for parents. It is generally agreed that personal advice of any kind is most often heeded when it is specifically sought. The doctor's contribution to the content of health education by teachers is important.

Congenital heart disease must be recognised at the entrant medical examination. The need to repeat auscultation in order to identify cases missed at the entrant examination is not an acceptable reason for periodic routine examinations. Unheralded or asymptomatic rheumatic carditis is too rare nowadays to be a condition that also merits recurrent screening of cohorts of normal healthy children by auscultation of doubtful reliability.

Musculo-skeletal disorders and cerebral palsy are not often fatal in children of school age and do not often require admission to hospital for treatment. On the other hand, orthopaedic disorders are common among all age groups examined by school doctors. It would seem that the majority of these are developmental variants affecting the feet, legs and posture that are within the bounds of normality and have little if any effect on function. The deputy school medical officer for Hampshire[15] has produced convincing evidence of the superior effect of special 'Foot and Back Surveys' compared with routine medical examinations in identifying children likely to need treatment for these defects, although the school doctors in Eastbourne[13] found such surveys time-consuming and less rewarding.

Epilepsy is seldom first identified at routine medical examinations and represents less than one per cent of defects noted; diabetes and renal disease are not recorded separately on the school medical record card. Again, the school doctor has few opportunities materially to affect mortality from these disorders, yet by keeping a watchful eye on the children in school who are subject to

---

[15] Bacon, L. (1969). Medical Officer, 21 March.
[13] Annual Report of Principal School Medical Officer, Eastbourne (1968).

22

epilepsy, or to asthma, the school doctor may be instrumental in obtaining for some of them adequate medical treatment of their disorders.

There is accumulating evidence[16] that bacteriuria (usually but not always asymptomatic) occurs in approximately 2 per cent of school girls and is often associated with genito-urinary pathology. Urine culturing has been found to be feasible for school entrants and older children and it may be that it should become a routine screening procedure in girls. The routine examination of urine for protein and sugar has not so far been found to be a worthwhile procedure in school health service examinations.

The eighteen diseases or groups of disorders so far referred to (excepting accidents and respiratory diseases) are relatively uncommon; yet they account for 90 per cent of the deaths and three-quarters of the hospital admissions of school children. The great majority of these disorders are first recognised by general practitioners who either undertake or arrange for treatment. In contrast, they account for barely one-third of the defects recorded at routine school medical examinations. According to the age group, between 50 and 60 per cent of these defects affect the sensory-motor skills of vision, hearing and speech; skin; and to a small extent nutrition. They are more prevalent than the 18 diseases above (see Table IV) but they are seldom (excepting skin diseases) first recognised by the family doctor, they seldom require hospital admission and very rarely cause death. (The long-term objective of reducing mortality among adults should not be overlooked by the school doctor, however; and the nutritional status of the school child is important in relation to his subsequent health and may be modified for the better by the efforts of the school doctor.)

The disorders with the next highest prevalence rates to ear, nose and throat conditions and defects of vision, viz. learning difficulties (whether or not these are associated with mental retardation), psychiatric disorders and the problems associated with puberty and adolescence, are largely missed by all three branches of the health service until they reach crisis point, e.g. serious academic failure in school, intolerable behaviour, pregnancy, delinquency or even drug addiction.

One reason—but not the only reason—why these disorders do not feature more prominently among the defects observed at intermediate and school leaver medical examinations is that an examination by a doctor, apart from being unreliable, is not the best guarantee that all disorders will be found even if they are present. In one special study already referred to[9] after excluding defects of vision, 80 per cent of the remaining defects were not recognised by the current method of routine medical inspection. Many disorders cannot be detected by even the most accurate physical examination alone. For example, the diagnosis of epilepsy and asthma, as well as psychiatric disorder, unless they are witnessed by the doctor at an examination, depend in the first place upon a history which stems from the observations of parents and teachers. In fact, if a comprehensive medical examination has been carried out at the age of 5, rheumatic carditis is the only disease among those listed in Table III (which account for 90 per cent of the defects noted at periodic medical examinations at present) which may require physical examination by a doctor for recognition of its possible presence. Medical examination is clearly essential in the investigation of whether or not a suspected disorder is actually present but it is not essential in alerting a doctor

---

[16] Savage, D. C. L. et al. and Meadow, S. R. et al. (1969). Brit. Med. J., 12 July.
[9] The School Health Service Report of Study Group set up by Secretary of State for Scotland (1968). Scottish Home and Health Department.

TABLE IV

Prevalence rates of certain childhood disorders

Disorder	Rate per 1,000 children	Ages	Reference
Bronchitis and pneumonia ..	65	5–9 years	(a) Fry, J. (1961). The Catarrhal Child. Butterworths, London.
Asthma	23	9–11 years	(b) Graham, P. J. et al. (1967). Brit. J. Soc. Med. 21, 71.
	48	5–11 years	(c) Dawson, B. et al. (1969). Lancet, 1, 827.
Bacteriuria ..	21	5 years (girls)	(d) Savage, D. C. L. et al. (1969). Brit. Med. J. 3, 75.
	10	5–15 years (girls)	(e) Meadow, S. R. et al. (1969). Brit. Med. J. 3, 81.
Diabetes	1	9–11 years	(f) Rutter, M. et al. (1970). Education, Health and Behaviour. Longman, London.
Acquired heart disease	1	7 years	(f) above
Congenital heart disease	3	7 years	(g) Alberman, E. (1969). In: 'Concern'. No. 3, November. National Bureau for Co-operation in Child Care, London.
Spina bifida ..	1	5 years	(h) Annual Report of Chief Medical Officer, Department of Health and Social Security, 1969. H.M.S.O.
Other congenital anomalies ..	6	7 years	(g) above
Musculo-skeletal disorders ..	3	9–11 years	(f) above
Cerebral palsy ..	3	5–14 years	(i) Rutter, M. et al. (1970). A Neuro-psychiatric Study in Childhood. Heinemann Medical Books, London.
Epilepsy	8	5–14 years	(i) above
Tonsillectomy ..	70	5–6 years	(j) The Health of the School Child, 1958 and 1959. H.M.S.O.
Inflammatory disease of ear ..	150	6 years	(a) above
	50	9 years	
Impaired hearing (30 dcb. loss both ears) ..	20	9–11 years	(f) above
Squint	35	7 years	(k) Alberman, E. et al. (1971). The Practitioner, Vol. 206, 501.
Impaired vision (6/12 or less in best eye) ..	100	9–11 years	(f) above
Marked speech defect ..	27	5 years	(l) The Health of the School Child, 1964 and 1965. H.M.S.O.
Mental retardation	26	9–11 years	(f) above
Educational retardation ..	79	9–11 years	(f) above
Psychiatric disorder	68	9–11 years	(f) above
Illegitimate birth and abortion ..	2	12–15 years	(m) Annual Report of Chief Medical Officer, Department of Health and Social Security, 1968. H.M.S.O.

to the possibility of its presence. The use of other screening procedures (i.e. procedures such as vision testing in schools which aim to do no more than reveal the possibility of there being a disorder) have not yet been sufficiently explored by the school health service. With suitable safeguards they would be preferable if they could be shown to be no less effective than the personal examination of a child by a doctor; there is reason to believe, however, that they may be more effective within their limited scope.

Tasks for the School Health Service

From what has been said, it is clear that the school health service is already complementing the other health services in the recognition of disorders and handicapping conditions. The tasks of the school doctors and the developments in the service that appear to be necessary may be more precisely stated as being:

(i)   to watch over the growth and development of the child attending school, not overlooking that his home environment may affect his health and his pattern of development at school, and vice versa;

(ii) to identify children with specific disorders that may affect their learning and behaviour, especially in the school situation and especially in so far as these may not reveal themselves to parents as conditions requiring referral to the family doctor (the chief disorders in this group are defects of vision, hearing and speech, and neuro-psychiatric disorders; the majority of the problems these cause in child management and teaching arise from the less obvious disorders and those of only moderate severity; the importance of such neuro-psychiatric disorders is not always appreciated and few school doctors have yet acquired through training the competence to examine for them or to play a significant part in their management);

(iii) to identify physical defects (especially those for which children are not usually taken to see their family doctor) at examination on entry to school;

(iv) to carry out population screening procedures for disorders which may not have a great effect on learning or behaviour in school, but which lend themselves to identifications by such procedures (for example, orthopaedic defects, cleanliness and certain skin disease);

(v)   to establish liaison and communication with schools, interpreting to the teachers the educational significance of what doctors may know about a child and are able to offer in the way of treatment (this function is still under-developed but there is no doubt of its importance);

(vi) to supervise in school children with disorders that usually receive treatment from general practitioners or hospitals but which have important implications regarding psychological development and education (the prevalence of epilepsy and asthma in school children is sufficiently high, and the occurrence of associated effects on learning and behaviour are sufficiently common, for these two disorders to be picked out for special attention in school);

(vii) to supplement arrangements for treatment of a child who may need more help than the other health services can usually provide (such treatments include speech therapy, physiotherapy, psychotherapy, and they may have an important long-term effect in preventing secondary handicaps);

25

(viii) to assist in the maintenance in school children of an adequate level of immunity to certain communicable disease;

(ix) to advise on health education programmes in schools;

(x) to supplement the advisory services for parents regarding the management at home of handicapped children, especially those with mental or neurological disorders since these children are often not attending a medical service when first admitted to school;

(xi) and to provide a consultation service for adolescents in secondary schools as a preventive measure to help the difficulties these pupils have in relation to psycho-sexual adjustment, drug-taking and other health matters;

(xii) and to work closely with family doctors and paediatricians.

A Pattern of Surveillance

Most of these tasks need to be undertaken in or in association with the school. The arrangements for the surveillance of children in school have now to be considered in the light of the criticisms that have been made of routine and selective medical examinations currently in use, and the outstanding problems in health and development.

(a) *Entrant Medical Examinations*

The lynch-pin of the arrangements for the surveillance of pupils is still a full examination of the child around the time of his first admission to school. The time has not yet arrived when the surveillance of children during the pre-school years is sufficiently comprehensive and widespread throughout the country to dispense with a routine examination of all school entrants; even when such a time does come there will always be a need for the last examination before five to be particularly related to the major event of entry to infant school.

The entrant examination should comprise a parent questionnaire for certain information concerning the child's social situation, his past medical history and the family history; a summary of relevant findings at pre-school medical and developmental examinations, and of immunisations; an assessment of the child's physical growth, including measurements of height and weight; a test of vision, and a clinical test of hearing, speech and language in addition to a screening test of hearing by pure tone audiometer; physical examination, including tests of fine and gross motor function and visuo-motor co-ordination; and a general assessment of the child's social and emotional development from behaviour observed and reported; and perhaps a culture of the urine of girls.

A teacher questionnaire is necessary when entrant medical examinations are arranged for children after their admission to infant school.

The parents can usually say what is happening about treatment of any disorder the school doctor may find and he will need to consider the appropriate action. Certain features of the child's physical state (e.g. his level of nutrition) or of his behaviour development may need to be discussed with the parent, who may need to be advised. Teachers also will need advice about any disorder or characteristic of the child that may be pertinent to the care and instruction of the child in school. Such information may be instrumental in modifying the attitude and expectations of the teacher with regard to children with developmental deviations likely to effect their learning and behaviour. If the head teacher can attend the entrant medical examination, discussion (with discretion in the presence of the child) between the doctor, the teacher and the parent may be exceedingly helpful to the teacher as well as reassuring to the parent. The doctor should visit the class teacher and see the children working in their classroom.

(b) *Follow-up Visits to the Schools*

Whether the entrant medical examination is carried out just before or after the child has reached school, certain children will be recognised whom the doctor will wish to see again shortly or about whose progress he will wish to enquire. The teachers may also have children about whom they would like to talk to the doctor again. Close surveillance of the children during their first year in school is an important service task.

(c) *Subsequent Medical Examination on Request*

The evidence available indicates that the special examination of a child on request from a parent, teacher or some other person is the most appropriate examination to provide for the continuing surveillance of children once they are in school. It is the most rewarding kind of examination for identifying most defects, including those miscellaneous disorders not specified separately in Table III, and for identifying at an early stage those defects which have arisen since entry to school. If the school health service is to be mindful of the efficiency of its methods, it cannot disregard the extent to which routine medical inspections record for the second or third time defects known to have been present at an earlier examination. The combination of a comprehensive entrant examination and special examinations on request has the added advantage that it makes minimal demands on the doctor as a screener and maximal demands upon him as a diagnostician and medical adviser.

(d) *Periodic Parent Questionnaire*

For the fullest use to be made of such a special examination and consultation service, both parents and teachers will need to be informed about it and briefed as to its objectives. This is basically an exercise in public relations. The co-operation of teachers especially will depend quite reasonably on the benefits they derive; and school doctors will have to be prepared to spend more time discussing the import of their findings with teachers and parents.

When the child approaches the age of 8 and 11 parents who have not previously requested an interview might be asked if they have anything concerning the health and development of their child about which they would like to talk to the school doctor. This may be done when asking all parents to answer a short questionnaire (3 or 4 questions only) about his health and about his behaviour at home since he started school; the object of asking about his behaviour would be the early recognition of the desirability of further investigation of this and/or of discussing his management with the parents. Care should be taken to enquire of significant illness or problems in care since the previous enquiry and not to repeat requests for information already provided at an earlier date.

The fact that the doctor finds no defect in a child whose parents asked for another examination should not be regarded as a criticism of the system of

27

examinations on request nor as evidence that the examination was a waste of time. Two recent surveys[6,8] have drawn attention to the fact that many parents of both normal children and those with physical or mental handicaps are concerned about the progress of their child in school as well as the cause of the disorder that may be present. Even if their concern is ultimately found not to be really warranted by the facts of the situation, the reassurance of the parents is an important and worthwhile task for the doctor. Quite often it will be found that the parents have rightly been concerned.

(e) *Periodic Screening Procedures*

The following five screening procedures might be carried out at certain intervals during school life:

test of visual acuity:
> this should be done annually or every other year;

test of hearing:
> opinion varies as to how often hearing should be tested by pure tone audiometric screening but perhaps it should certainly be done at approximately the ages of 7, 10 and 13;

measurement of height and weight:
> these also could be done at the same ages, the percentile readings at entry to school and at 7 being an aid to assessing the medical need for free milk to be provided during the middle school years;

survey of feet and back, of skin, and of hygiene:
> these should be arranged not less frequently than every three years, as the child reaches the ages of 7, 10 and 13;

cleanliness survey:
> as considered necessary in certain schools or in selected areas.

(f) *Advisory Service for Adolescents*

As an aid to the early recognition of mental and physical problems associated with adolescent adjustment, and as a preventive measure for young people still attending school, the school doctor should seek to establish an advisory service in the secondary schools, attending for a session at regular intervals so that pupils may make their personal appointments to see him. Such sessions have already been arranged in a few schools and they have helped to meet a very real need.

The Rôle of the Nurse in Surveillance

It is customary for the school nurse to carry out tests of visual acuity and cleanliness in almost every local education authority, but she is seldom asked to help in other screening procedures. However, her rôle might well be extended. For example, she might with advantage undertake screening tests of hearing with the pure tone audiometer. Her knowledge of the schools and the children is an asset, it would add still more variety to her work as well as rounding it off, and the

---

[6] Middlemiss, T. and Ward, J. A. (1961). Scottish Home and Health Dept., Vol. XXVI, No. 2.

[8] Tizard, J., Rutter, M. and Whitmore, K. (1970). 'Education, Health and Behaviour'.

schools would have one less person with whom to have to liaise than when somebody else does it.

The school nurse could also extend the scope of cleanliness inspections so that, as already happens in some authorities, she could undertake a hygiene survey, including an inspection for skin disease. Feet are also inspected by some school nurses in special surveys; with little more trouble these hygiene surveys could include an inspection not only of skins but also of backs, particularly of secondary school children.

The nurse should also be more than a receptionist at the entrant medical examination. In two authorities in which comprehensive examination of children during their first term in school is being carried out as part of a wider study of the profile of school entrants in an educational priority area, the nurse is completing a parent questionnaire when visiting the child's home, in the normal course of her duties, and explaining to the parent the purpose of the examination and the need for the parent to be present. As well as testing the children's vision, she records their height and weight and various other measurements, and the height of the mother, and she takes an active part in the neuro-developmental tests. It has been found that the nurses appreciate this greater involvement, which adds interest to their work as well as being of more assistance to the doctor.

In-service training of school nurses, of the kind already a standard practice in some authorities (see Health of the School Child, 1966–68), is necessary if they are to be more involved in medical surveillance of school children, and such training will need to include practice in observation and in other techniques beside vision testing. The reliability of vision testing by school nurses is known to be high and there is no reason why this should not be the case with other screening procedures. A check on their continuing reliability would be necessary but this is required today in respect of vision testing and it is required of all persons (doctors not excepted) concerned with routine procedures carried out on a largely normal group of children, e.g. medical examinations and pure tone audiometric screening.

Help from the Teachers in Surveillance

Teachers can assist in the surveillance of school children in two ways. The first is by completing a simple teacher questionnaire similar to the parent questionnaire referred to above. It has been shown that enquiries must be made of both parents and teachers if all children who may have a psychiatric disorder are to be recognised.

The second way that teachers can help is by arranging an educational screening test for children aged between 7 and 8. The object of this could be to identify still at a relatively early stage children with learning difficulties, including those associated with moderate mental retardation, not previously identified by neuro-developmental tests on entry to school. These tests are valuable in themselves but they have not yet been validated as predictors of subsequent educational retardation and in any case cannot be expected to forecast difficulties in every child who is backward in his middle school years. The most important educational screening test is the functional one of attainment and progress in the classroom. Only teachers can apply this test but school doctors and psychologists have the task of investigating those children who fail to achieve a certain level of competence at school.

The third way in which teachers can help is by bringing to the notice of the school nurse those children who are unduly often absent from school.

Organisation of the School Doctor's Work

Any such pattern of surveillance of school children as described above will depend for its success very considerably on the extent to which school doctors are known to parents and teachers and can help them. Neither of these conditions can obtain unless the doctor is a frequent visitor to the school. The tasks described provide ample reason for such visits, and if it is the intention of school doctors to concentrate on the identification during the school years of disorders which interfere especially with a child's function in any field of activity at school, the best way to do so is to observe the child functioning in the classroom, gymnasium or playground.

It is often claimed that if the school health service is to maintain even the minimum statutory requirement of three medical inspections of pupils the shortage of school doctors only allows two or three days, or less, per annum in any school according to the number of pupils attending and that two or three days per term is quite impossible. Apart from the fact that so many routine inspections are no longer statutory, a review of the amount of medical time allocated to such inspections can lead to redeployment of the doctors on priority tasks. Even if it is felt that three medical examinations are necessary for proper surveillance, spreading examination sessions over the terms instead of having them in blocks of a few days once a year has advantages, especially regarding the image of the service and its impact on the school even though there may be administrative disadvantages. It is a common experience that teachers do not usually maintain their objections to frequent medical sessions in the school if this gives them the kind of help they need from the school doctor.

Frequent visits to a school need not mean that each visit has to be for a full session of two to three hours. Shorter visits may be all that is required on some occasions, and at some schools, especially the small village schools. It is exceedingly difficult, and hence time-consuming, for administrative staff to plan the school doctors' programmes for such frequent, short visits but there is no necessity for them to do so. School doctors often complain that they do not have time to call in at their schools because their time-tables are so tightly scheduled with fixed sessions at clinics or schools, planned in advance without their co-operation. It is understandable that a school health service should wish to organise routine medical inspections in such a way that no pupil is overlooked and it might, therefore, welcome a reduction in the number of such inspections and the consequent reduction in complicated administrative arrangements. However, there are alternative methods of organising medical examinations that do not depend upon the school doctor's weekly programme being planned in the central office. For example, the method in Oxfordshire is for the health visitor/school nurse to make the arrangements for medical examinations in school to suit the head teacher and the general practitioner (see Health of the School Child, 1964/65). There is no reason why the same method should not be used in schools in other authorities in which the school doctor carries out the examinations; many of the doctors would welcome the opportunity to provide in their own way the service required by the schools for which they are responsible. It is appropriate that responsible people like school doctors and nurses should have delegated responsibilities of this kind. No doubt the liberation of the school health service from the obligation to provide the Department with statistical data based upon the Medical Record Form 10 M would go some way to enabling such a major administrative change to occur; this is a matter that the Working Party on the Medical Record Form will need to consider in their review of the pilot use of the Revised 10 M.

The comments of a school doctor taking part in a Foot and Back Survey have implications for the school health far beyond the identification of children with orthopaedic defects: 'We learned a great deal during the Foot and Back Survey. We noticed in 1964 and subsequently that the children from social problem families were unattractive; this means that their posture was poor, their clothing was inappropriate and not particularly clean, their movements were ungraceful, altogether they appeared to be without specific defects but not as one expects and finds good citizens, or the children of good citizens.

'I think even a good PE mistress would have found it difficult in that particular school to help the girls of poor physique, the majority of whom came from homes with poor standards so that the girls were absent from PE or had excuses including letters not uncommonly written by the girls themselves.

'This social handicapping I came to realize was far more important than a defect of the type categorized by Form 10 M.

'If the School Medical Officer is accepted by the Head Teacher and the staff, one could help the staff in dealing with these somewhat deprived children and the Hampshire selective procedure did enable one to use one's time for the benefit of the teaching staff and so, I believe, for the school children.'

CHAPTER III

MENTALLY HANDICAPPED CHILDREN

The Education (Handicapped Children) Act received the Royal Assent on 23 July 1970 and the Secretary of State appointed 1 April 1971 as the date from which the Act operated.

The Act abolished the duty originally laid upon local education authorities by Section 57 of the 1944 Education Act of ascertaining which children were unsuitable for education in school on account of a disability of mind. Consequently, from the appointed day local education authorities ceased to have power so to classify a child and local health authorities ceased to have power under Section 12 of the Health Services and Public Health Act of 1968 to make arrangements for the training of mentally handicapped children of compulsory school age. Responsibility for the education of all school children, whatever the nature and extent of their handicap, now lies with local education authorities and from 1 April 1971 those children between the ages of 2 and 16 who prior to that date had been reported to a local health authority under Section 57 of the 1944 Education Act have been regarded as handicapped pupils who were ascertained to be such under Section 34 of the Act.

Background to the Change in the Law

Under Section 36 of the 1944 Education Act parents have always had a duty to arrange for their child to receive '. . . efficient full-time education suitable to his age, ability, and aptitude . . .' and under Section 37, a local education authority has a duty to require parents to satisfy it that the child is receiving such education if it has reason to doubt this. However, local education authorities often found themselves in a predicament in operating Sections 37 and 57 in a consistent manner since they appeared to be based upon conflicting concepts: one, that all children should receive education according to their age, ability, and aptitude; the other, that some children with extremely limited ability and aptitude are unable to benefit from education in school and need treatment in a training centre. Education and training were never defined for the purposes of the Acts. The Royal Commission on the Law Relating to Mental Illness and Mental Deficiency, in its report published in 1957, described the objective of training as being '. . . habit training, teaching the children to keep themselves clean and to feed and dress themselves, sense training to improve alertness, movement and speech, and carefully graduated handwork of all kinds . . . reading, writing and arithmetic (for) those who are thought to be able to develop even a rudimentary understanding of writing and figures.' The Commission went on to say that '. . . most of this is the equivalent of the nursery training of a very young normal child, and when this is the type of training which an older child needs it may more appropriately be considered a health service than an education service.'

Developments in the education of severely handicapped pupils gave rise to doubt whether this was an appropriate division of responsibility, whilst a clearer understanding of the specific intellectual disabilities of severely subnormal children led to experiments in teaching which indicated that such children's learning could be enhanced by a more structural approach than was customary. The problem facing local education authorities was that of reconciling these points of view with classification of a child as unsuitable for education in school. Some authorities resolved their difficulties by arranging for the admission of a child to a training centre following informal agreement with the parents and the local health authority. The parents naturally welcomed such informal arrangements since the changes in the operation of Section 57 by virtue of the Mental Health Act, 1959, never entirely removed the unnecessary distress that formal ascertainment caused. What the new Act does primarily is to remove the requirement of local education authorities to ascertain whether a child is unsuitable for education in school before arranging for him to receive the kind of education most likely to meet his needs according to his age and very limited ability and aptitude; implicit in this repeal of Section 57 is the acknowledgment that the administrative distinction between training and education is no longer meaningful in this field.

It is against this background that school doctors need to view the change in the law. At the same time a note of caution needs to be sounded. A change in designation of an educational establishment from training centre to special school and transfer of responsibility for its administration from one department of a local authority to another does not overnight produce startling effects on the developmental progress of mentally handicapped children. There should be full recognition of the contribution that training centres have made towards meeting the problems of families with a mentally handicapped child and the achievements of the staff in helping individual children. The major benefits to mentally handicapped children that may be expected in the future are the long-term ones that follow from advances in teaching and management; these are largely dependent upon the lessons learned from painstaking research into the disabilities and needs of the children which have then to be incorporated into the training of teachers and doctors. The Education (Handicapped Children) Act, 1970, opens the way for further advances in this field of special education and ensures that no source of educational or medical expertise is denied the children and teachers concerned. Indeed, it is possible that the greater involvement of local education authorities in the education of mentally retarded children may have important repercussions on the special education of less handicapped children who prior to 1 April 1971 were classified as ESN pupils.

Immediate Effect of the New Act

As from 1 April 1971 a child who before that date might have been examined under Section 57 because of a known or a suspected mental disability is examined, like a child with any other handicap, under Section 34 of the 1944 Education Act, to determine his need for special education. If it is then necessary to classify the child in terms of the categories defined in the Handicapped Pupils and Special Schools Regulations, 1959 (and this is by no means always necessary unless Form 1 HP has to be completed), he should be regarded as E.S.N. There is no provision in the new Act for a new category of severely subnormal pupils to be defined, and it is hoped that the children will cease to be described as such whilst they are in schools. The terms 'severely subnormal' and 'mentally subnormal' do not cease to have relevance because of the 1970 Act, but they were

33

defined for use mainly in a social context for the purpose of the Mental Health Act, 1959, and are inappropriate in an educational context. It is preferable that school children whose level of intelligence is about two standard deviations or more below the mean should be referred to as mentally handicapped, a description already widely accepted by their parents and one that is comparable to that of physically handicapped and equally appropriate for children with a mild or a severe handicap. This practice might eventually result in doctors and teachers ceasing to equate educational subnormality so closely with mental subnormality and paying more attention to the need for, and the methods of providing, special education for seriously educationally retarded children who are not mentally handicapped.

The Act provided for existing staff, buildings and other facilities that local health authorities had made available in junior training centres, to pass to the local education authorities. Circular 15/70 issued on 22 September 1970,[1] requested local education authorities to consider, with local health authorities, for which establishments they would assume responsibility on the appointed day. It was anticipated that local education authorities would normally propose that existing junior training centres be approved by the Secretary of State as special schools for E.S.N. pupils, and this has generally proved to be the case. In a few instances, it has been proposed that separate junior training centres should be amalgamated with existing E.S.N. special schools. On 31 December 1969, there were 302 separate junior training centres. There were another 80 junior training centres which were part of all-age centres; the Circular drew the attention of local education authorities to the need for an administrative division to be made between the junior and adult sections to allow for the establishment within the premises of a recognisable special school.

By the end of 1969, local health authorities had provided 211 special care units for children who were severely physically handicapped or very disturbed in their behaviour, as well as being mentally handicapped. (In a special survey of the children in thirteen special care units carried out by the Department of Health and Social Security in 1968, almost one-third of the children were non-ambulant, one in six had suffered from epilepsy during attendance at the unit, and 4 per cent were hyperkinetic; a similar proportion were blind and almost as many were deaf.) One hundred and seventy-three of these special care units were sited in junior training centres and 38 were in separate premises. It is anticipated that the majority of the latter will operate independently, either as E.S.N. special schools or on the lines of the special classes and units which already exist within the provision now made by local education authorities for special education. A few special care units may be associated either with existing special schools or those that used to be junior training centres.

By 31 December 1969 local health authorities had provided 68 hostels with accommodation for 1,286 mentally handicapped children. One-third of the places were for children who lived too far from a junior training centre to attend daily from their own homes and who needed weekly boarding facilities. The greater number of places were for children who for one reason or another needed more permanent placement. Most of the hostels offering weekly boarding facilities and closely associated with a former training centre passed to local

---

[1] Responsibility for the education of mentally handicapped children.

education authorities; the remainder were taken over by the new social services departments of local authorities.

Besides those children who attended training centres or special care units, there were some severely mentally handicapped children who were in-patients in subnormality hospitals, either on a long-term or short-term basis. Reports indicated that about half these children attended hospital school full time and the rest remained in their wards all day. Under the Act, no child of compulsory school age is outside the scope of the education system, and children in sub-normality hospitals need to be given teaching appropriate to their needs (save in the exceptional circumstances of an illness which for a time might render any child medically unfit to attend school). The extension of educational facilities to children in subnormality hospitals has taken a variety of forms, including the establishment of more special schools in the hospitals and the attendance of children at local special schools outside the hospitals. Teaching on the wards has been necessary for some children at first but it is hoped that eventually most children will have a special school room to go to for some periods daily.

Wherever mentally handicapped children are placed, where the local education authority is providing education, the full range of the school health services and the school psychological services are available to them. The medical rôle continues to be especially important in diagnosis and assessment as before but it also encompasses continuing surveillance of the children in their special schools as well as certain treatment facilities, such as speech therapy. The relationship between the school health service and the medical staffs of the hospitals must, of course, become increasingly close and hospital staff should be associated with work outside their hospitals.

Prevalence of Severely Mentally Handicapped Children of School Age

When comprehensive and reliable surveys of the prevalence of severely mentally handicapped children (IQ under 50) have been undertaken in selected areas, a figure in the region of 3·7 per 1,000 of the 2–15 age group has usually been arrived at.

On 31 December 1969, the number of mentally handicapped children under the age of 16 known to local health authorities, and their placement, were as follows:

18,311 children were attending 302 junior training centres;
3,754 children were attending 80 junior training centres within all-age centres;
2,281 children were attending 173 special care units sited within junior training centres;
780 children were attending 38 separate special care units;
7,711 children were attending as in-patients in subnormality hospitals;
1,340 children were attending independent establishments.

34,177

This group of children represents 3·3 per 1,000 of the 2–15-year-old child population. However, the two prevalence figures quoted are not strictly comparable. Whilst the great majority of the 34,177 children are likely to have been

35

ascertained under Section 57 of the 1944 Education Act as unsuitable for education in school, this is not to say that they all had IQs under 50; it is known that some children in training centres and subnormality hospitals have an IQ above 50. Furthermore, a certain number of the children were under the age of 2. Thus, the number of severely mentally handicapped children known to local authorities falls appreciably short of the number that might be expected.

The addition of 32,837 children who were attending junior training centres, special care units and subnormality hospitals to the category of E.S.N. pupils increases the number of handicapped pupils attending or awaiting admission to special schools to approximately 145,000, making two-thirds of the special school population E.S.N. pupils.

Recommendations for Special Education

The Education Act, 1944, places upon local education authorities the responsibility for deciding which children require special education. In reaching a decision an authority is dependent upon professional advice in the form of reports from those who know the child or have examined him. In practice, a medical report is one of the most important single factors determining an authority's decision, and to obtain this report the authority has power under the Act (Section 34 (1)) to require the child to be medically examined.

The key rôle of the school doctor in an authority's decision is most clearly evident in those cases in which the local education authority considers it in the interests of the child to proceed, in spite of parental objection, with a proposal to place the child in a special school; this it cannot do unless the child has been examined in the manner set out in Section 34 of the 1944 Education Act, the doctor has issued a Form 1 HP to parent or authority if either so requests and the parent has been informed of his right of appeal to the Secretary of State. In completing Form 1 HP the examining doctor is required not only to state the nature and extent of the child's disability but also to certify in which category of handicapped pupil the child should in his opinion be placed. These categories are defined in terms of special educational need but it is medical opinion that principally governs an authority's decision that the child needs special education —at least in the sense that under the particular circumstances quoted, an authority could hardly pursue a special school placement without a medical statement that the child is a handicapped pupil. In fact, an authority rarely does so, even when there is no objection to the proposal by the parent.

The crucial importance of the information obtained from a full medical examination in arriving at these decisions is not at all in question, but it does not give unquestioned pre-eminence to medical opinion in determining how a handicapped child needs to be taught and consequently, as a rule, where he should be taught.

When a child has either an auditory, visual or physical disorder the importance attached to medical opinion regarding the need for special education is perhaps understandable, since medical treatment may be an integral element in it. However, when the disorder is severe the educational implications are obvious and when it is only mild or moderate what teachers most want to know is the extent of the handicap and the degree of adjustment to it that may be expected, so that they may judge for themselves the teaching the child requires. The situation is rather different when the child has a mental disability. Medicine has very little in the way of treatment to offer the majority of mentally handicapped children, once a diagnosis has been made or attempted, unless a physical disorder such as a visual or hearing defect is also present. Also, parents of mentally handicapped children, in contrast to those of physically handicapped children, have much greater difficulty in accepting that their child is handicapped, and far more often object to local education authorities' proposals for the child to attend a special school or a training centre. It is, therefore, unfortunate that in just these delicate situations formal ascertainment is so frequently resorted to and the school doctor cast in an authoritarian rôle. It is true that some authorities have adopted the procedure of offering parents a place for their child in a special school principally on the basis of reports and recommendations from teachers or educational psychologists; and a few have gone so far, perhaps unwisely and certainly unnecessarily, as to dispense with any medical information until after the admission of the child. Furthermore, a small number of other authorities have arranged for a team of school doctor, psychologist and teacher to advise on the educational placement of handicapped children. Nevertheless, most local education authorities still adopt formal ascertainment procedures, requiring the school doctor to carry out a full statutory examination of the child and to complete Form 2 HP before they are prepared to offer a child a place in a special school whether or not teachers and psychologists have already recommended this and the parent has agreed to it. A few authorities go to the length of requiring the medical officer to complete a Form 1 HP on every child examined, and in spite of the injunction under Section 34(5) of the 1944 Act.

Formal ascertainment procedures in which the doctor is given the principal rôle often places him in the embarrassing position of either appearing to rubber-stamp an educational recommendation made by a teacher or education psychologist or vetoing it, in which case the parent is understandably confused. It can also lead to a situation in which the relationship between doctor and parent is irretrievably upset. This is especially undesirable in those cases in which parents and authorities disagree regarding the special education of the child, since the doctor can fulfil an important intermediary rôle if he is not seen as the instigator of the authority's decision. Also, in these and other cases, there is often a continuing need for the school doctor to be in a position to advise and support parents in the handling of their mentally handicapped child; this he cannot do if he does not have the confidence and trust of the parents. He can also discuss the child's needs with the family doctor to whom the parents may go. The reasons for the adherence of local education authorities to formal ascertainment and their dependence on medical recommendations are not far to seek. Partly, it is because the importance of medical diagnosis is fully appreciated; partly, also, because of the administrative convenience of forestalling the situation that can arise if the parent does not accept the authority's proposal regarding special education following an examination that has been carried out informally. The power given to local education authorities, under the Mental Health Act, 1959, to take action under Section 57 of the 1944 Education Act if this proved necessary after an examination arranged formally under Section 34, was a further disincentive to examine mentally handicapped children under informal arrangements. Above all, however, it is because for at least 50 years the power of local education authorities to provide special education for mentally handicapped children was dependent in law upon certain procedures of medical certification. This is an odd survival in view of the great reduction in formal certification in

37

psychiatric services generally. The Education Act, 1921, directed that children '. . . not being imbecile and not being merely dull and backward . . .' should be provided for in special classes and schools; thus it was necessary first that they be certified as feeble-minded, and this was a medical responsibility. The 1944 Education Act reversed this procedure by requiring local education authorities to exclude from the education system, by reporting to the local authority for the purpose of the Mental Deficiency Act, 1913, children who had been found incapable of receiving education in school. It was still the doctor who had to certify on Form 2 HP that the child had a disability of mind such as to render him ineducable or to make it inexpedient for him to be educated with other children. The Mental Health Act, 1959, made certain modifications to terminology and procedure to encourage a more tolerant and sympathetic attitude towards children with mental disorders but it is only through the operation of the 1970 Education (Handicapped Children) Act that the education services are required to assume responsibility for the education of every mentally handicapped child, without the label of certification. In this they have of course taken on the further development of services, initiated by health authorities with the advantages of a specifically educational approach.

Paradoxically, it is only as a result of the repeal of Section 57 of the 1944 Education Act that it may ultimately be appreciated how school doctors, in effect, have been operating a selection procedure on behalf of local education authorities for the admission of mentally handicapped children to special schools. From 1 April 1971, unless changes are made in the manner in which school doctors report and make recommendations following the examination of mentally handicapped children, the more severely handicapped will not be differentiated either by name or by category of school from the less handicapped children needing full-time special education as E.S.N. pupils; both groups will be classified by the school doctor as E.S.N. and recommended for special school placement, when this is considered necessary. The authority will then need to choose between offering the child a place in the school which has always been known as the E.S.N. school and in that which used to be known as the junior training centre, where this continues to be a separate establishment. The selection of a school has always been the prerogative of educational staff. It has not been customary for school doctors to recommend placement in particular schools and it would be unfortunate if a precedent were set in the case of mentally handicapped pupils. Instead, the process of rationalising the rôles of the doctor and the educationist in the ascertainment of handicapped children, already started by the Education Act of 1970, should be taken to its logical conclusion, and this should then be the basis for new procedures for arranging special education for E.S.N. children.

It is often overlooked that in the clinical context the question of whether or not a child is E.S.N. is virtually decided by the teacher, at the time of initial referral; if the child were not so educationally retarded that his needs could normally be provided in the ordinary school his teachers would not have referred him. It should not be necessary for the school doctor to confirm or deny this in the administrative context, and largely on the basis of a measure of the child's intelligence, before the teacher's request for help is met. It is, of course, for the doctor to determine whether there is some other reason than mental handicap for educational retardation and, where appropriate, to take action to remove it. Educational retardation should be regarded as a symptom. The medical function is then to investigate the reasons and to make a diagnosis. This is part of a process of assessment to which the educational psychologist should also contribute. From the nature and extent of any disability found, which must be carefully explained to the teacher, a plan for education must be worked out; this is principally an educational function, though the doctor should be able to offer advice. How and where the child's education is best arranged, and whether he should be educated as a handicapped pupil, is also a matter for which an educationist should be principally responsible for advising the authority, though again the doctor should be able to make some useful suggestions, especially if there is associated physical disability. Many of the problems that arise from formal procedures of ascertainment can be avoided by doctor, teacher and educational psychologist contributing their particular professional expertise to a joint assessment procedure resulting in a carefully considered, widely based joint recommendation to the authority, which should be a prescription for education rather than a classification of the child.

Appeals to the Secretary of State

Under Section 57 of the 1944 Education Act, parents had a right of appeal to the Secretary of State against a proposal of the local education authority to report their child as unsuitable for education in school. The procedure for dealing with such appeals in the Department, and the frequency and outcome of appeals during the ten years 1951–1960, were given in the Health of the School Child, 1960–1961. Section II of the Mental Health Act, 1959, came into operation in November 1960, and modified certain legal procedures and simplified administrative arrangements relating to the examination of children under Section 57.

TABLE *summarising the outcome of appeals under Section 57 of the 1944 Education Act, for the years 1951–1969*

	Number children reported per annum (1)	Number parents appealed per annum (2)	Col. (2) as percentage of (1) (3)	Number children examined per annum (4)	Col. (4) as percentage of (2) (5)	Number parents supported per annum (including LEA withdrawal) (6)	Col. (6) as percentage of (2) (7)
1951 ..	3,157	369	11·6	[32]	—	6	1·6
1952 ..	3,294	371	11·2	114	30·7	16	4·3
1953 ..	3,149	325	10·3	98	30·1	8	2·4
1954 ..	3,010	362	12·0	118	32·6	17	4·7
1955 ..	2,863	287	10·0	82	28·5	13	4·5
1956 ..	2,782	277	10·0	104	37·1	16	5·7
1957 ..	2,675	233	8·7	77	33·0	7	3·0
1958 ..	2,725	291	10·6	114	39·1	17	5·8
1959 ..	2,784	247	8·8	90	36·8	10	4·0
1960 ..	2,777	212	7·6	88	41·5	20	9·4
1961 ..	2,739	215	7·8	63	29·3	51	23·7
1962 ..	2,729	217	7·9	81	37·3	60	26·7
1963 ..	2,569	166	6·4	62	37·3	39	23·5
1964 ..	2,667	162	6·1	65	40·0	37	22·8
1965 ..	2,633	172	6·5	54	31·4	43	25·0
1966 ..	2,623	155	5·9	35	22·5	30	19·3
1967 ..	2,624	158	6·0	31	19·5	29	18·3
1968 ..	2,555	153	6·0	23	15·0	25	16·3
1969 ..	2,229	139	6·2	20	14·3	31	22·2

Since one of the intentions of the 1959 Mental Health Act was to encourage a more sympathetic and less restrictive attitude towards the management of people with mental disabilities, it was expected that there might be fewer occasions when local authorities might feel obliged to report a child as unsuitable for education in school in spite of the parents' objections, and consequently fewer occasions on which parents might want to exercise their right of appeal. The accompanying Table shows that there has been a steady reduction in the number of children reported each year under Section 57 as unsuitable for education in school, and that this trend had already started in 1953. Allowing for the increase in the number of children in maintained primary and secondary schools over the same period, the rate of reporting under Section 57 has actually fallen by half, from 5·8 per 10,000 pupils aged 2 to 15 years in 1951 to 2·9 in 1969. Similarly, the proportion of parents appealing to the Secretary of State against such reporting has fallen yearly from 11·6 per cent in 1951 to 6·0 per cent each year since 1966.

In the nine years up to 1959, almost one-third of children who were the subject of an appeal were examined by one of the Department's medical officers prior to a decision by the Secretary of State. In 1960, and again in 1964, as many as 40 per cent were so examined. During the last three years, however, there has been a marked reduction in this number to approximately one in seven.

The most striking change since the 1959 Mental Health Act came into operation has been the greater number of occasions on which parents have been upheld in their appeal. Since 1961, 345 parents have been successful in their appeals. This represents 22 per cent of the total number appealing, and includes 218 cases in which a decision in favour of a parent was made by the Secretary of State and 127 cases in which the local education authority withdrew its proposal as a result of the parent initiating an appeal.

The repeal of Section 57 of the 1944 Education Act, as from 1 April 1971, saw an end of appeals under this section, but it is unlikely that it will also bring an end to disputes between local education authorities and parents regarding the education of severely mentally handicapped children. Enquiries have shown that approximately four out of five parents of such children have been well satisfied with the placement of their child in a training centre, and there is no reason to suppose that they will be less satisfied as a result of the transfer of responsibility for the training centres from local health to local education authorities. It may be, therefore, that only a small minority of parents may strongly disagree with a proposal to place their child in an E.S.N. special school that was formerly a training centre; the issue will then be one of choice of school and a matter to be dealt with under Section 37 of the 1944 Education Act.

Under Section 37(3) of the Act, if the authority considers the school selected by the parent is not suitable for the child and the parent does not agree with the authority's choice of school, it '. . . may, after giving to the parents notice of their intention to do so, apply to the Minister for a direction determining what school is to be named in the order.' Before making any such direction the Secretary of State invariably invites the parents to justify their own choice of school. Parents do, therefore, have an opportunity of stating their case, although it is not until a later stage when a school attendance order is in force and the local education authority refuse to comply with the parents' request for a change in the school or a revocation of the order that they have a right of direct appeal to the Secretary of State, as laid down by Section 37(4) of the Act.

CHAPTER IV

PHYSICALLY HANDICAPPED CHILDREN

The changing pattern of physical handicaps has been referred to in previous editions of the Health of the School Child and it is interesting to note that the number of children with spina bifida in special schools continues to rise by approximately 200 per year. In many special schools for the physically handicapped the number of children with spina bifida has equalled, or exceeded, that of children with cerebral palsy, but in others the increase has not been so dramatic and may be related to an unexplained patchy distribution of the condition throughout the country, as well as to local differences in policy of admitting the physically handicapped to suitable ordinary schools.

The numbers on the registers of special schools for delicate and physically handicapped pupils in January 1968, 1969 and 1970 are summarised in Table I. The increase is mainly, though not wholly, due to spina bifida. There were also in January 1970, 143 physically handicapped children attending special classes or units attached to ordinary schools full-time and a further 26 children attending part-time.

Education of the physically handicapped, especially those with a motor handicap, requires co-ordinated action by a team which includes both the health professions and the teachers. The child is taught in the classroom, receives physiotherapy in another room, and may receive speech therapy and perhaps occupational therapy in another part of the building. If in a boarding school, he is cared for out of school hours by the house-parents. Ideally there is respect and understanding of the rôle of each professional so that one may find teachers and the physiotherapists taking part in out of school activities or all the therapists lending their skill to the difficult task of encouraging those severely affected by cerebral palsy to try to feed themselves. In the boarding school the important part played by the non-professionals—caretaker, driver, handyman, cook and domestic staff—may be underestimated. Co-operation and co-ordination between the different professions is nowhere needed more than in the school for the physically handicapped. It has been suggested that every special school for the physically handicapped should have a social worker attached so that the child's social needs as well as his physical, educational and emotional needs may be kept in balance and all possible links with his home maintained. At present much of the work of liaison with home falls on the headmaster and his staff.

Haemophilia

During the past decade great strides have been made in the treatment of haemophilia, Christmas disease and the other similar, but rare, bleeding disorders. It can fairly be claimed that if doctors, parents and those responsible in the special day and residential schools ensure that the children with haemophilia receive efficient treatment promptly there is now far less risk that they

TABLE I

England and Wales—Number of physically handicapped pupils in special schools

	1968			1969			1970		
	Boys	Girls	All Pupils	Boys	Girls	All Pupils	Boys	Girls	All Pupils
Cerebral palsy	1,514	1,251	2,765	1,536	1,234	2,770	1,631	1,313	2,944
Spina bifida	493	553	1,046	618	685	1,303	701	832	1,533
Muscular dystrophy	435	70	505	433	88	521	478	76	554
Haemophilia	177	—	177	186	—	186	189	—	189
Post-poliomyelitis	223	219	442	213	162	375	165	151	316
Heart disease—congenital and rheumatic	373	335	708	395	347	742	366	338	704
Congenital deformities of limbs	243	199	442	230	139	419	257	216	473
Perthe's disease	105	29	134	104	26	130	131	23	154
Other physical handicaps	1,216	792	2,005	1,220	898	2,118	1,288	844	2,132
Total	4,779	3,448	8,227	4,935	3,629	8,564	5,209	3,793	8,999

will grow up with crippled limbs and joints. Previously the frequent episodes of bleeding, prolonged spells in hospital and consequent erratic education led to difficulties in obtaining and keeping employment.

Haemophilia is a hereditary disease resulting from a deficiency of a clotting factor in the blood and is present at birth, but attention is usually drawn to it in early infancy by the presence of extensive bruising or prolonged bleeding from small cuts on the body. Once the diagnosis has been made at one of the haemophilia centres in the hospital service a special card is issued giving vital information such as the name, address and telephone number of the general practitioner, the telephone number of the haemophilia centre at which the patient is registered, his blood group and other important physical details. This is a standard national card issued through the haemophilia centres and should be carried at all times. Special arrangements may be made by the centre for the speedy transfer of the patient either to the centre or hospital in which he receives treatment.

It is not perhaps generally realised that none of the sons of a haemophilic man will have haemophilia or be able to pass the disease, but that all his daughters will be carriers of the disease. Half of the daughters' sons may have haemophilia and half of the daughters' daughters may be carriers and capable of passing haemophilia on to their sons. At present it is not possible, before the birth of a haemophilic son, for the daughter of a carrier mother to know whether or not she is a carrier herself. A sister of a haemophilic man has a fifty per cent chance of not having inherited the defect or of being a carrier, in which case half her sons may have haemophilia and half her daughters may be carriers and pass it on to their children.

Pain, fear and insecurity play a large part in the life of a boy with haemophilia. Haemorrhages into joints and muscles in haemophilia can be very painful and this can be lessened by refraining from unnecessary movement and initiating treatment as soon as possible by a transfusion of human plasma, freeze dried human anti-haemophilic globulin concentrate (AHG) or cryo-precipitate prepared from human plasma. This replacement therapy raises the concentration of factor VIII (in haemophilia) or factor IX (in Christmas disease) to a level which is high enough to arrest bleeding while healing occurs. Care should be taken not to give pain killing drugs containing aspirin, the use of which is contra-indicated in haemophilia.

Because of the complexity of the treatment and rarity of the disease full use should be made of the specially designated centres but the management of a school child with haemophilia will involve close co-operation of all concerned, the doctors, nurses, physiotherapists, teachers and social workers with the parents. At the Lord Mayor Treloar College, Alton, Hampshire, up to fifty boys with haemophilia or similar conditions are maintained and have the advantage of specialist medical care either at the local hospital or in the well equipped and staffed sick-bay at the school, where their treatment is supervised by a research fellow in haemophilia who also has close links with the haemophilia centre in Oxford.

Spina bifida

Spina bifida, unlike some other disabilities, is usually immediately apparent at birth and may involve surgery in the neonatal period and repeatedly in the pre-school years. This introduces an immediate problem in helping parents to acceptance and understanding of their child's disability. That this should be sustained is vital not only to keeping the child as a member of his own family and community, but also to ensure that progress made at school may be maintained.

The load borne by parents of a severely handicapped child is onerous indeed and they need not only direct help in sustaining it, but a special effort at understanding by those who advise them. When the residential nursery block at Coney Hill, Kent, run by the Shaftesbury Society, was opened in 1967 rooms where parents may stay for training were included. Other schools provide a well equipped caravan in the grounds for use by parents. If trophic sores or urinary infections are allowed to develop during the holidays much valuable time, needed for education, will be wasted when the child returns to school. Measures should, therefore, be taken, with the agreement of parents, to ensure that there is a follow up of professional care during holidays through the general practitioner and hospital staff. It may be considered advisable to ask that a district nurse, health visitor or local school nurse should visit to supervise dressings or medication. It is, of course, helpful for there to be a two-way flow of information between the general practitioner at home and at the school so that each may be kept informed of any illness or change in the child's physical or mental condition. Problems of this kind are common to many of the major handicaps, but they are specially prominent in spina bifida.

Experience gained over the past two or three years has reinforced the appreciation of the need for early educational experience and particularly the continued involvement of parents in the care of their child, if he is in a hospital,

43

nursery, special or ordinary school. It is generally accepted now that early surgery will improve the chances of survival for babies born with meningomyelocele; the quality of survival, however, is still felt by some experts to be a matter for conjecture. Regular periodic reassessment of the child's medical, educational and social needs will encourage the maximum social integration, intellectual and physical development within the limits of his disability. Satisfactory mental adjustment to the handicap is a key factor in determining the child or young person's limitation of activity and underlines the need for an awareness of the problem and intelligent observation of the child by all concerned with his education. A simple example may be the finding, not after all surprising, that these children, and others with a physical handicap, tend to become obese. While this may be an indication of some emotional upset as well as enforced inactivity, it undoubtedly adds to their social and educational problems in that they become too heavy for parents, or staff, to lift and more likely to be confined to their wheelchairs or to need admission to a residential instead of a day school. They may also have an increased tendency to develop trophic ulceration of the skin. A balanced, but restricted, diet is needed for these children.

There is now more awareness of the problems of the complications of meningomyelocele for which a balance of skills in the care of the child is needed; the neuro-surgeon, urologist, orthopaedic surgeon, paediatrician, general practitioner and school medical officer, are all concerned as well as the physiotherapist, occupational therapist, teacher and educational psychologist. The urological programme will include the management of infection, ensuring the free evacuation of urine as well as the recognition and early investigation of retention of urine which would produce back pressure and ultimately destruction of the kidneys and renal failure. Chronic renal disease may be associated with hypertension, the incidence of this increasing with age. In many special schools regular measurements of blood pressure form part of the examination of any child with urinary incontinence and meningomyelocele. Anaemia may be a further complication. Orthopaedic surgeons and physiotherapists will endeavour to ensure that the child is ambulant or at least standing by the age of about 3 years old. Lumbar kyphosis and chest deformities are frequently associated with meningomyelocele.

There is a high incidence of complications in the ventriculo-venous shunt (Spitz-Holter valve), and all in charge of these children at school, or at home, should be aware of the symptoms of early blockage or raised intracranial pressure so that skilled treatment may be obtained immediately. The early observation that a child is 'off colour' or lethargic, not eating, shunning light or noise, or complaining of a headache, and not wanting to play, should be an alarm signal because vomiting, the appearance of a squint or the occurrence of a fit may indicate an established cerebro-spinal hypertension. The sudden appearance of a squint in a previously non-squinting child with a Spitz-Holter valve inserted calls for immediate specialist investigation to avert the possible disaster of the development of optic atrophy.

Conclusion

It is to be hoped that the intensive medical care and special education which the pupils with severe and multiple physical handicaps receive at special schools will enable most to obtain a rewarding and interesting occupation on leaving school and to be as independent in the activities of daily living as is possible within the limits of their disabilities. For some, however, there will need to be hostel provision to ease the transition from school, for others some form of community care will be appropriate. Others may be able to pursue an academic career at a university, at a non-maintained establishment for the further education and training of the disabled or, at the Hereward College for the Further Education of the Physically Handicapped at Tile Hill, Coventry, which accepted its first students in September 1971 and has close links with the ordinary college of further education on the same site as well as with other colleges in Coventry and with local industry.

During the last few years at school the encouragement of a realistic outlook to job potential and appreciation of the difficulties of meeting and competing with those from a less sheltered background can be of immense benefit to the physically handicapped school child.

CHAPTER V

SURVEY OF PHYSICALLY HANDICAPPED
CHILDREN IN ORDINARY SCHOOLS

History

In September 1969 a letter was sent to all the principal school medical officers in England and Wales enlisting their help in obtaining information, for the first time, about physically handicapped children attending ordinary schools. This survey was initiated by Dr. Peter Henderson when he was the Department's Senior Principal Medical Officer and it was felt that it would be valuable to have an overall picture of the type and severity of the children's handicap as well as the specialist medical or nursing services which have been, or need to be provided for them. It was hoped, also, that the results of the computer analysis would indicate, amongst other things, how many of these physically handicapped children have more than one disability which may influence their ability to benefit fully from education.

A small survey limited to principal school medical officers in the Midlands and North Midlands, in 1963, showed that out of a school population of approximately 1,000,000, there were 156 physically handicapped children in ordinary schools. Many of these children were severely handicapped; 16 being in wheelchairs, 28 used calipers or crutches and 18 were incontinent.

Towards the end of 1950 a questionnaire was sent to each principal school medical officer in England and Wales with the object of discovering how many physically handicapped children were considered to require education in special schools. The results also revealed that in a school population of around 5,970,000 approximately 16,719 pupils were known to be physically handicapped and 8,476 were in ordinary schools. During the past 20 years there has been a dramatic reduction in the number of children with deformities due to infection, such as poliomyelitis, osteomyelitis or tuberculosis of bones and joints but an increase in those handicapped as a result of congenital defects and accidents.

Method

The survey involved the completion of 2 questionnaires and it was appreciated that although there was unlikely to be a large number of physically handicapped children in ordinary schools in any one Authority, nevertheless, it would involve the medical officer and some of his colleagues in a considerable amount of work.

Form A was to be completed in respect of each maintained school with physically handicapped pupils on the roll and gave an indication of a type of school and frequency of visits by school doctors, nurses and therapists.

A copy of Form B was completed for every child included in the survey and asked for details of the nature of the defects, and, amongst other things, the provision of mobility and other aids, physiotherapy, speech therapy, transport to and from the school and the presence of incontinence.

There was no attempt to enquire into the suitability of the educational placement or the child's progress in the ordinary school.

It soon became evident from some of the returns submitted that considerable doubt existed about the definition of 'physically handicapped' children for the purpose of the survey. A further letter was therefore sent to the principal school medical officers explaining that information was only required about those physically handicapped children who had one, or more, of the conditions listed in section 8 of Form B, for whom special additional attention is required in the school or who are unable for long periods to take a full part in all normal activities of children of their own age.

Out of a total of 163 local education authorities in England and Wales (146 in England, 17 in Wales), 148 authorities participated in the survey. The results from 147 authorities went through the computer; one large county submitted the results too late for inclusion by the end of the summer term 1970.

General Difficulties Encountered in the Survey

There were obvious differences of opinion among doctors about the criteria to be adopted in diagnosing a child as physically handicapped.

Shortage of staff was given by several local authorities as a reason for delay in returning the forms or failure to take part in the survey. Others suggested that the information would be difficult to obtain.

It has been assumed, perhaps over-optimistically, that the handicapped children placed in ordinary schools would be known to, and periodically reviewed by, a senior medical officer of the authority and that it would only be necessary to pick out the physically handicapped from a register or file kept for this purpose.

There are regional variations depending, to some extent, on the availability of day special school provision and whether it is in an urban or rural area.

In general the medical officers took a great deal of time and trouble to ensure that accurate information was given and enlisted the help of school nurses and teachers. There were some forms, however, where the information given was so badly written that it could not be deciphered, where conditions other than those specified in the instructions had been given, or the information was incomplete, inaccurate or otherwise worthless. In some cases it appeared doubtful if they had been scrutinised by a medical officer.

It was impossible to show the degree of handicaps, for example, the diagnosis of cerebral palsy could include the 'clumsy child', the hemiplegic with learning difficulties or the severely athetoid child.

It is not possible to draw definite conclusions from the numbers given in many of the tables; one child may appear under several different headings as in Tables I and II where a child with cerebral palsy may have a heart defect and scoliosis and appear under these headings.

The survey does, however, indicate certain definite trends in the type and severity of the disabilities.

Results

The following table shows the prevalence of the disabilities in the various types of school. The majority of the 10,200 children are in primary schools.

47

Survey of physically handicapped children in ordinary schools
1969–70 (England)

Disability	1 Nursery	2 Primary	3 Sec. Mod.	4 Grammar	5 Other maintained secondary	6 All secondary	7 All maintained schools
Limbs; upper, lower, talipes and dislocated hips ..	11	1,675	361	81	260	702	2,388
Heart defects— rheumatic or congenital ..	5	1,435	300	78	293	671	2,111
'Others'	7	930	240	69	249	558	1,495
Cerebral palsy ..	15	1,005	253	37	152	442	1,462
Spina bifida ..	5	598	100	22	64	186	789
Post poliomyelitis ..	—	140	191	53	148	392	532
Perthe's disease ..	—	344	60	7	45	112	456
Muscular dystrophy and atrophy ..	2	189	40	12	21	73	264
Achondroplasia and other forms of dwarfing	3	184	37	7	22	66	253
Hydrocephalus; without myelomeningocele	2	210	20	2	12	34	246
Haemophilia and Christmas disease	—	152	40	20	32	92	244
Scoliosis	3	126	39	17	41	97	226
Amputations: upper and lower limbs ..	—	109	48	15	32	95	204
Rheumatoid arthritis	—	103	41	24	31	96	199
Osteomyelitis ..	—	52	18	4	19	41	93
Fragilitas ossium ..	—	44	9	2	11	22	66
Tuberculosis of bones and joints.. ..	—	11	8	—	7	15	26
Total (Disabilities)	53	7,307	1,805	450	1,439	3,694	11,054

The category of 'others' contains small groups of a wide variety of defects including some rare hereditary conditions and a few where the diagnosis indicated a progressive deterioriation during childhood and it would seem that an ordinary school had been chosen so that the child might remain in his home surroundings.

The preponderance of heart defects is surprising. If the forms have been completed correctly these children should have a significant heart lesion, or congenital abnormality, and not just a functional heart murmur causing little or no disability. No valid inference can be drawn about the current incidence of cardiac abnormalities in childhood from these figures but the successful results of the new techniques in cardiac surgery will result in more children being able to attend ordinary school and many, who previously would have died, being enabled to live useful lives. It is interesting, however, that in the previously mentioned survey which took place in 1950, heart disease or defect (congenital and rheumatic) was the most frequently recorded pathological condition followed by cerebral palsy, deformities and amputations of limbs, poliomyelitis, tuberculosis, spina bifida and muscular dystrophy.

The total distribution of disabilities throughout the range of maintained schools is as follows:

Nursery Schools	0·48% of the total number of physically handicapped children in ordinary schools
Primary Schools	66·10% of the total number of physically handicapped children in ordinary schools
Modern Schools	16·33% of the total number of physically handicapped children in ordinary schools
Grammar Schools	4·07% of the total number of physically handicapped children in ordinary schools
Other Secondary Schools	13·02% of the total number of physically handicapped children in ordinary schools
All Secondary Schools	33·42% of the total number of physically handicapped children in ordinary schools

The small percentage in nursery schools may in part be due to the fact that the children are below the age of compulsory school attendance and many may be in day nurseries or other day provision.

The number of physically handicapped children in special schools, in England, and their disabilities is given in the table overleaf for comparison during the period covered by the survey.

Table I shows that the majority of the 10,200 children are in primary schools. This is not unexpected because it is the period when difficulties involving mobility are not so great. It may be noted that 119 children with spina bifida and a ventriculo-venous shunt, or Spitz-Holter valve, are in ordinary primary schools and are included in the total of 603 children with spina bifida in primary schools. Most of these children need considerable medical supervision and help from a physiotherapist and school nurse. There is little difference between the number of boys with haemophilia in special and ordinary schools.

Table II indicates that out of a total of 10,200 physically handicapped children included in the survey, 8,176 had no additional defects; 1,837 had one additional defect; 178 had two additional defects; 9 had three additional defects and none had four additional defects. 19·84% of children with one disability had also additional defects, particularly those with spina bifida, cerebral palsy and fragilitas ossium. The presence of these additional handicaps confirms the general impression and experience gained in special schools where the majority of children have multiple handicaps.

Number of physically handicapped pupils in special schools (England)

Nature of handicap	1969			1970		
	Boys	Girls	All pupils	Boys	Girls	All pupils
Cerebral palsy ..	1,489	1,198	2,687	1,573	1,259	2,832
Spina bifida ..	600	672	1,272	668	799	1,467
Muscular dystrophy	415	88	503	460	73	533
Haemophilia ..	184	—	184	189	—	189
Post poliomyelitis	212	160	372	162	150	312
Heart disease— congenital and rheumatic ..	391	344	735	361	333	694
Congenital deformities of limbs	214	186	400	249	211	460
Perthe's disease ..	98	21	119	124	21	145
Other physical handicaps ..	1,133	846	1,979	1,082	831	1,913
Total	4,736	3,515	8,251	4,868	3,677	8,545

Table III. Incontinence is often said to be a bar to a child attending an ordinary school because he is not socially acceptable. This table would seem to be open to some misinterpretation because one would not necessarily expect children of 5 years and under to have gained full control of bowel and bladder. If 'an appliance' has been correctly interpreted as a urinary bag for boys or a bag fitted after an ileal loop operation for girls the resulting figures seem to be much higher than would seem probable. The table appears to show that 21 boys and girls were incontinent at 16 years and over (11 wearing appliances) and 8 were still doubly incontinent.

Table IV is a record of the number and types of mobility and other aids used by the children in the categories of disability listed in Section 8 of the questionnaire. It had been hoped that the computer would be able to give information about whether a hearing aid had been provided for those children considered to need one and whether it was worn 'all or most of the time'; 'some of the time' or 'not at all', but this was not found to be possible. Neither was it possible to equate those children in classrooms needing assistance with feeding, toileting, dressing or using stairs with those actually receiving this extra help.

Table V gives details of children using prostheses. The majority of these are children with congenital limb deformities, including many where the deformity may be attributable to Thalidomide, and those who have had amputations as a result of accidents.

Table VI. Many physically handicapped children require regular help from a physiotherapist and speech therapist to enable them to benefit from education. This is particularly important early in their school life for those with spina bifida and paralysed lower limbs and for children with cerebral palsy and difficulty in communication. It is disturbing to note that 128 children needing physiotherapy and 122 children needing speech therapy were not receiving it.

An attempt was made on Form A, which was sent to each school taking part in the survey, to ascertain the frequency of visits by medical officers, school nurses, physiotherapists and other professionally concerned with handicapped children. From the returns submitted it was obvious that these questions gave

TABLE I

Survey of physically handicapped children in ordinary schools (England) 1969–70
Handicapped pupils by type of ordinary school

Nature of handicap	Nursery		Primary		Modern		Grammar		Other maintained secondary		All maintained schools		Direct grant and independent		All schools	
	Special unit	Not in special unit	Special unit	Not in special unit	Special unit	Not in special unit	Special unit	Not in special unit	Special unit	Not in special unit	Special unit	Not in special unit	Special unit	Not in special unit	Special unit	Not in special unit
Cerebral palsy	2	13	30	975	6	247	—	37	2	150	40	1,422	—	6	40	1,428
Spina bifida	1	2	3	302	—	70	—	16	—	43	4	433	—	—	4	433
Myelomeningocele with SHV	1	—	9	109	—	2	—	—	—	2	10	113	—	1	10	114
Myelomeningocele without SHV	—	—	—	174	—	28	—	6	1	18	1	227	—	2	1	229
Post poliomyelitis	—	1	1	137	—	190	—	53	1	147	2	527	—	—	2	527
Heart defects—rheumatic, congenital	—	—	3	1,423	1	297	—	78	1	292	5	2,095	—	1	5	2,096
Haemophilia and Christmas disease	—	5	12	148	3	40	—	20	1	32	16	240	—	—	16	240
Muscular dystrophy and atrophy	—	—	4	186	—	40	—	12	—	20	4	260	—	4	4	264
Limbs—upper, lower, talipes, dislocated hips	—	2	3	1,665	—	360	—	81	1	256	4	2,372	—	9	4	2,381
Amputation—upper limbs, lower limbs	1	10	—	109	1	48	—	15	1	32	3	204	—	—	3	204
Perthe's disease	—	—	—	341	—	60	—	7	—	45	—	453	—	—	—	453
Rheumatoid arthritis	—	—	3	102	—	41	—	24	—	31	3	198	—	—	3	198
Fragilitas ossium	—	—	1	44	—	9	—	2	—	10	1	65	—	—	1	65
Achondroplasia and other forms of dwarfing	—	3	4	180	1	36	—	7	—	22	5	248	—	2	5	250
Osteomyelitis	—	—	4	52	1	18	—	4	—	19	5	93	—	—	5	93
Tuberculosis of bones and joints	—	—	—	11	—	8	—	—	—	7	—	26	—	—	—	26
Hydrocephalus without myelomeningocele	—	—	4	206	—	20	—	—	—	12	4	242	—	—	4	242
Scoliosis	—	2	1	125	—	39	—	17	—	40	2	224	—	1	2	225
Others	—	7	13	917	4	236	—	69	3	246	20	1,475	—	4	20	1,479
All children	5	45	91	6,604	13	1,651	—	425	9	1,332	118	10,057	—	25	118	10,082

NOTE: Since some children suffer from more than one disability, the numbers in the vertical columns may be greater than the numbers given against the heading 'all children'.

TABLE II

Survey of physically handicapped children in ordinary schools (England) 1969–70
Handicapped pupils with additional defects

DISABILITY	No additional defect	1 additional defect — Incontinent	1 additional defect — Speech defect	1 additional defect — Hearing defect	1 additional defect — Visual defect	1 additional defect — Total	2 additional defects — Incontinent plus speech	2 additional defects — Incontinent plus hearing	2 additional defects — Incontinent plus visual	2 additional defects — Speech plus hearing	2 additional defects — Speech plus visual	2 additional defects — Hearing plus visual	2 additional defects — Total	3 additional defects — Incontinent plus speech plus hearing	3 additional defects — Incontinent plus speech plus visual	3 additional defects — Incontinent plus hearing plus visual	3 additional defects — Speech plus hearing plus visual	3 additional defects — Total number of children	All 4 additional defects	Total (Y)	Total no. of pupils with one or more additional defects (X)	X as a % of Y
Cerebral palsy	1,030	35	126	12	211	384	7	1	8	8	23	3	50	2	—	1	1	4	—	1,468	438	29·84
Spina bifida	250	130	—	2	29	161	2	1	21	—	1	—	25	1	—	—	—	1	—	437	187	42·79
Myelomeningocele with Spitz-Holter valve	30	73	1	—	6	80	—	—	14	—	—	—	14	—	—	—	—	—	—	124	94	75·81
Myelomeningocele without Spitz-Holter valve	95	100	2	1	16	119	—	—	14	—	1	1	16	—	—	—	1	1	—	231	136	58·87
Post poliomyelitis	462	5	2	—	60	67	—	—	2	—	1	—	3	—	—	—	—	—	—	532	70	13·16
Heart defects—rheumatic, congenital	1,824	17	41	6	206	270	2	—	4	2	6	4	18	—	—	—	—	—	—	2,112	288	13·64
Haemophilia and Christmas disease	220	1	4	—	19	24	—	—	—	—	—	—	—	—	—	—	—	—	—	244	24	9·84
Muscular dystrophy and atrophy	222	9	9	—	25	43	—	—	—	—	1	1	2	—	—	—	1	1	—	268	46	17·16
Limbs—upper, lower talipes, dislocated hips	1,985	93	47	4	224	368	3	1	18	2	16	1	41	2	—	—	1	3	—	2,397	412	17·19
Amputation—upper and lower limbs	175	3	1	2	23	29	—	—	—	—	—	—	—	—	—	—	—	—	—	204	29	14·21
Perthe's disease	405	4	2	1	43	50	—	—	—	—	1	—	1	—	—	—	—	—	—	456	51	11·18
Rheumatoid arthritis	180	—	3	2	14	19	—	—	—	—	—	—	—	—	—	—	—	—	—	199	19	9·55
Fragilitas ossium	50	6	—	1	9	16	—	—	—	—	—	—	—	—	—	—	—	—	—	66	16	24·24
Achondroplasia and other types of dwarfing	208	6	5	1	31	43	1	—	—	—	3	—	4	—	—	—	—	—	—	255	47	18·43
Osteomyelitis	80	2	—	—	9	11	—	—	—	—	—	2	2	—	—	—	—	—	—	93	13	13·98
Tuberculosis of bones and joints	25	—	—	—	1	1	—	—	—	—	—	—	—	—	—	—	—	—	—	26	1	3·85
Hydrocephalus without myelomeningocele	165	17	4	1	51	73	—	—	3	—	3	1	7	—	1	—	—	1	—	246	81	33·93
Scoliosis	182	7	8	—	29	44	—	—	—	—	1	—	1	—	—	—	—	—	—	227	45	19·82
Others	1,161	103	51	11	138	303	3	1	10	7	6	4	33	1	1	—	2	2	—	1,499	338	22·55
All children	8,176	500	263	35	1,039	1,837	18	4	77	14	53	12	178	5	1	1	2	9	—	10,200	2,024	19·84

TABLE III

Survey of physically handicapped children in ordinary schools (England) 1969–70

Incontinence

Age	BOYS					GIRLS				
	Bladder only	Bowel only	Both bladder and bowel	Total	Number wearing appliance	Bladder only	Bowel only	Both bladder and bowel	Total	Number wearing appliance
5 and under	17	3	24	44	12	19	2	24	45	13
6 ..	28	9	27	64	18	23	2	27	52	27
7 ..	22	6	17	45	19	27	2	22	51	17
8 ..	17	8	16	41	18	18	3	7	28	9
9 ..	20	3	8	31	13	19	2	9	30	15
10 ..	9	2	12	23	9	9	1	9	19	10
11 ..	14	2	11	27	11	7	2	2	11	5
12 ..	11	1	4	16	5	9	3	3	15	8
13 ..	10	1	4	15	8	10	3	2	15	11
14 ..	9	—	2	11	7	5	1	3	9	5
15 ..	6	4	3	13	6	7	1	3	11	5
16 and over	9	1	5	15	8	2	1	3	6	3
Total	172	40	133	345	134	155	23	114	292	128

53

54

TABLE IV

Survey of physically handicapped children in ordinary schools (England) 1969–70

Aids provided—All aids

DISABILITY	Number using wheelchair		Number using a walking aid (any)	Number using 1 or more prostheses	Number using hearing aid	Number receiving personal assistance (Ques. 12)	Number wearing glasses	All children [in survey]
	Electrically operated	Hand operated						
Cerebral palsy	—	47	161	17	28	403	247	1,468
Spina bifida	1	55	125	19	4	122	51	437
Myelomeningocele with Spitz-Holter valve	1	61	81	9	—	94	20	124
Myelomeningocele without Spitz-Holter valve	—	39	99	9	2	93	31	231
Post poliomyelitis	—	13	260	14	—	61	63	532
Heart defects—rheumatic, congenital	—	11	15	16	12	106	220	2,112
Haemophilia and Christmas disease	—	11	18	2	—	16	19	244
Muscular dystrophy and atrophy	4	49	32	11	1	134	27	268
Limbs—upper, lower, talipes, dislocated hips	4	80	428	363	11	444	260	2,397
Amputation—upper and lower limbs	1	10	34	163	2	33	23	204
Perthe's disease	—	13	199	9	2	68	44	456
Rheumatoid arthritis	—	6	17	3	2	32	14	199
Fragilitas ossium	—	8	11	1	1	15	9	66
Achondroplasia and other types of dwarfing	—	2	7	3	3	44	34	255
Osteomyelitis	—	1	14	—	—	6	10	93
Tuberculosis of bones and joints	—	1	3	—	—	2	1	26
Hydrocephalus without myelomeningocele	—	12	26	1	1	56	58	246
Scoliosis	—	2	52	5	1	48	30	227
Others	1	41	112	38	27	237	159	1,499
Total children	10	383	1,482	597	73	1,748	1,185	10,200

TABLE V

Survey of physically handicapped children in ordinary schools (England) 1969–70
Aids provided—Prostheses

DISABILITY	Number of children using the following prostheses								Total number of children using prostheses
	1 Arm	1 Leg	2 Arms	2 Legs	1 Arm 1 Leg	1 Arm 2 Legs	2 Arms 1 Leg	2 Arms 2 Legs	
Cerebral palsy	1	3	—	1	—	—	—	—	5
Spina bifida	4	5	1	—	—	—	—	—	10
Myelomeningocele with Spitz-Holter valve	—	—	1	—	—	—	—	—	1
Myelomeningocele without Spitz-Holter valve	—	2	—	1	—	—	—	—	3
Post poliomyelitis	2	6	2	1	—	—	—	—	8
Heart defects rheumatic, congenital	1	4	2	1	—	—	—	—	8
Haemophilia and Christmas disease	—	—	—	1	—	—	—	—	1
Muscular dystrophy and atrophy	—	—	—	—	—	—	—	—	—
Limbs—upper, lower, talipes, dislocated hips	187	96	11	32	7	3	—	2	338
Amputation—upper and lower limbs	44	99	1	18	—	—	—	1	163
Perthe's disease	—	2	—	1	—	—	—	—	3
Rheumatoid arthritis	1	—	1	—	—	—	—	—	2
Fragilitas ossium	—	1	1	—	—	—	—	—	1
Achondroplasia and other types of dwarfing	—	—	—	—	—	—	—	—	—
Osteomyelitis	—	—	—	—	—	—	—	—	—
Tuberculosis of bones and joints	—	—	—	—	—	—	—	—	—
Hydrocephalus without myelomeningocele	—	—	—	—	—	—	—	—	—
Scoliosis	—	1	—	1	—	—	—	—	1
Others	7	12	1	—	—	—	—	—	21
All children	233	188	15	62	7	3	—	3	501

55

TABLE VI

Survey of physically handicapped children in ordinary Schools (England) 1969–70
Services provided
Provision of physiotherapy, transport and speech therapy

Physiotherapy

Number requiring physiotherapy				Number receiving physiotherapy			Number requiring but not receiving physiotherapy
	Of whom the following number suffer from						
Total	Cerebral palsy	Spina bifida or myelomeningocele	Haemophilia or Christmas disease	at school	at hospital	elsewhere	
1,222	480	156	15	71	730	301	128

Transport

Number requiring transport	Provided with transport				Not provided with transport
	by bus	by taxi	by car	by ambulance	
Children a. in wheelchairs b. using walking aids c. using leg prostheses					
698	92	319	192	8	89
Other children [including those using other aids]					
1,115	322	436	277	13	79

Speech therapy

Number requiring speech therapy	Number receiving speech therapy	Number requiring but not receiving speech therapy
356	234	122

56

rise to some confusion and few had any clear pattern of visits. The table below may not give a true picture because children may have been attending for therapy at a hospital or clinic.

Services provided—number of schools receiving visits (England)

	Daily	Weekly	Monthly	Twice a term	Every term	Yearly	Less fre- quently	Not at all
Medical officer	1	125	434	521	1,681	2,979	207	158
School nurse	61	930	1,452	1,079	2,047	307	69	161
Educational psychol- ogist ..	1	64	253	445	1,099	977	1,757	1,510
Speech therapist	5	259	27	81	332	463	1,174	3,765
Physio- therapist	2	45	15	4	8	34	306	5,692
Remedial teacher ..	2	96	30	15	3	—	1	5,959
Audo- metrician	—	10	4	14	145	593	75	5,265
Peripatetic teacher ..	7	38	17	21	40	52	101	5,830
Nursing auxiliary	1	53	25	34	91	19	8	5,875

Conclusion

It is the wish of many parents that their child should attend an ordinary school, both for social and educational reasons. In Circular 276, issued on 25 June, 1954 by the Department of Education and Science it states that 'no handicapped pupil should be sent to a special school who can be satisfactorily educated in an ordinary school.' Where a special school is necessary, a day school is preferable if it offers a satisfactory and practical solution.

It has been shown that 10,200 physically handicapped children are, in fact, attending ordinary schools. For some this may be the right placement but for others the more sheltered environment of the special school with smaller classes, intensive medical and nursing care and a full range of therapies available may be more suitable. Those in the special schools tend to be the most severely physically handicapped; many having multiple defects.

This survey by its very nature and the inclusion of multiple observers and many variables can only produce a value judgement which cannot be standard- ised. It may, however, be considered to be an indication that further study of the needs of physically handicapped children in ordinary schools might be appropriate.

CHAPTER VI

HOME TUITION

The following is a summary of the observations made on some of the 40 children seen by one of the medical officers of the Department of Education and Science whilst they were having home teaching.

This gave an excellent opportunity to review the total situation and to discuss problems with the child, parent and teacher. The children lived in a major county borough, where there were good special school facilities, and also in the neighbouring county.

Reasons for recommending home tuition included temporary home teaching during a convalescent period after leaving hospital and before returning to school, severe handicap impeding daily travelling to school, parents' refusal of residential education, and severe emotional problems expressed as school phobia.

Medical assessment was carried out by the school medical officer either in the child's home or in a Local Authority Clinic. In the majority of cases either the Health Visitor or School Nurse had contact with the home.

Home tuition was not in all cases a suitable solution. One 5-year-old spastic girl with a speech defect was having home teaching in the only living room where her younger sisters were playing. She had been considered too difficult because of her speech defect and physical handicap for education in a special school for the physically handicapped and there was no vacancy in the school for spastics. One very bright little girl with mild spasticity was recommended home tuition for slight urinary incontinence. Ordinary school might have been possible with the aid of an incontinence pad. A child with a gastrostomy for congenital oesophageal atresia stayed at home all day with a neurotic severely depressed mother whose difficulties had been exacerbated by the child's illness.

The home teachers had little medical guidance either from the local authority doctor or from the family practitioner. If the doctors concerned had had the opportunity to reassess the children in their homes, working with the teachers, they would have benefited from the teachers' observations and knowledge of their pupils and the teachers would have gained more insight.

One boy who had been perfectly healthy until the age of 10 when he developed acute paralysis associated with spina bifida occulta was ashamed to use his calipers in front of his friends: his teacher, not knowing the full facts, was afraid to encourage him lest he should harm himself further.

A severely depressed adolescent boy apparently suffering from school phobia was educated by a brisk, extrovert woman who was well-meaning but had no insight into his problems and lacked any opportunity to discuss her pupil with the doctor; she saw him as a malingerer and was cold and unsympathetic.

One family was on the verge of breaking up because of difficulties presented by a severely handicapped, apathetic, depressed, adolescent boy with spina bifida. The family was completely controlled by his whims: he refused to be left alone in the house for even 10 minutes. His mother, who was severely crippled with rheumatoid arthritis was unable to lift the boy herself, the father could not, or would not, help and had threatened to leave home, so that the burden fell on his teenage sister, who had become resentful and frustrated. The teacher was the only one to counsel and support the family. Re-appraisal of the family was sadly needed. They lived in a council house midway up a steep hill with steps to the house and garden. Although the bathroom and lavatory were on the ground floor no mechanical aids had been provided to make the boy more independent: he had to be carried upstairs to bed by his mother and sister.

In sharp contrast to this family was one large family who, although materially poor, were united in their task of looking after a child of nine years, severely crippled, and dwarfed due to Still's disease which had been treated with steroids. There was no feeling of tension in this home: all members had their part to play. The older girls looked after the younger children while the mother nursed the handicapped child. The home teacher had found for some while that her pupil had been lethargic and disinterested in her lessons. The teacher had no medical contact with whom to discuss her observations. On examination the child was found to be febrile and losing weight. When questioned as to why she had not sought medical advice the mother replied that the child was often ill, but soon recovered: she then went on to say that she saw the paediatrician once a year and her family practitioner infrequently, the last time being two years before. The child died shortly afterwards.

An adolescent girl, midly dyspnoeic and cyanotic due to a congenital heart lesion, had always had home tuition. For the past year, since her mother's death, the girl had been at home by herself all day apart from visits from her home teacher and the occasional visit from a married sister. The teacher had taken her in her car to the neighbouring school for cookery and needlework. The girl also disclosed that she went by bus to town at weekends. When seen, this girl was severely depressed and it was difficult to see why the situation had been allowed to continue. There was no evidence that she had ever been medically reassessed in accordance with her emotional and social needs.

Similarly, an adolescent boy severely crippled with haemarthrosis was literally locked in the house with an aged deaf grandmother and a mother depressed following the death of her husband. The mother was very emotionally dependent on the boy whose only contact with his peer group was an occasional visit from a neighbour.

A very able adolescent girl who had had subacute endocarditis had been receiving home tuition since the age of 14 years. Having achieved 6 excellent 'O' levels at home, she was at the time of the visit studying for 'A' levels. She was shy and timid, arrested at the pre-pubertal level of emotional development. The only contact outside her immediate family was with a girl of her own age. There was no contact with anyone from the grammar school which she had previously attended.

There was evidence of delay in communication from the consultant to the local authority medical staff. One little girl, who had been recommended for home tuition while being treated for Perthe's disease, had had her plaster removed and was running about. The local authority had not been told that she was ready to return to school. Another child, who had been severely injured in a car accident, was advised to return to school by her consultant, but the mother, a tense, neurotic woman, had decided that home tuition should be prolonged because of the mental trauma the child had suffered.

There was also evidence that communication back to the consultant was inadequate. A bright, lively girl, gravely disfigured by blistering with scarring and alopecia caused by porphyrinuria, was recommended by her consultant to have home tuition in order to avoid the trauma of travelling in a car to school. Her father took her to town at the weekend without any obvious exacerbation of her condition. She also occasionally went out into the street to play. The question remained whether the benefit from companionship of children of her own age in the sheltered environment of a special school would have been worth the risk of trauma. A girl had been at home two years to avoid trauma following plastic surgery for facial burns: the neighbours said she regularly played in the street.

Children educated at home were isolated from the community. The mother of an adolescent girl severely crippled following poliomyelitis was embittered because her daughter had not been invited to the local school plays or Christmas activities. A boy with pseudo-hypertrophic muscular dystrophy had become more disabled by the time he was due to transfer to the comprehensive school and his parents had refused residential placement. There was no contact with the local school: he was neither invited to the school nor did children visit him at home. In contrast, in an area where the youth service was well developed a handicapped girl was visited by children of her own age: they came to play games or just to chat.

A paraplegic girl had been provided with mechanical aids and kitchen adaptation by the Local Authority. Her parents took her out in their car at weekends and she was welcomed by her relatives, but she, too, had no contact with her own age group, neither was she allowed to take her chair into the shops or cinemas.

Now that we are moving towards community participation there is an open field for the younger generation to be involved with young handicapped people who are unable to go to school, but need the help and companionship of their peer group to develop emotionally and socially.

CHAPTER VII

THE ASTHMATIC CHILD

The number of children suffering from asthma in England and Wales has been variously estimated at between 100,000 and 150,000. The number certainly does not appear to be less than 100,000. There are difficulties, however, in estimating the incidence of asthma in children because of the variety of diagnostic labels given to wheezy children, from bronchitis, wheezy bronchitis, to asthma. E.g. what relationships does wheezy bronchitis bear to asthma?

Incidence

The incidence appears to vary markedly from area to area. Williams and McNicol[1] recently reviewed this subject and found a variation in incidence throughout the world from 1% to 14%. The authors felt that it was not possible to say whether or not the incidence was rising but suggested that it was most likely that variations are due to different methods used in defining asthma, in sampling methods, and in examination techniques.

House Dust Mite

Since the review of asthma in the Health of the School Child, 1960 and 1961, a great deal has been learnt about the house dust mite as a cause of asthmatic attacks. The work of Voorhorst et al.[2] in 1964 has shown that the mite, dermato-phagoides pteronyssinus, and certain other species present in house dust can produce severe asthmatic attacks in allergic subjects.

D. pteronyssinus is a small mite found in house dust in almost all homes. It is most abundant in damp houses and during the period September to November. The mite appears to grow best at a temperature of 25°C, with a high humidity of about 80%, and preferably on human dander. These conditions are most readily found on, and in, mattresses, and as might be expected, the house dust mite content of dust from mattresses is higher than that of dust from other parts of a house. Individuals allergic to the house dust mite, will give a positive skin test to preparations of mite specific allergens. The method of skin testing is important and the prick test appears to be the most satisfactory. It is, therefore, important to aim at reducing as far as possible the amount of house dust in the homes of asthmatic subjects. The use of a vacuum cleaner helps to this end and vacuuming the mattresses also reduces the house dust mite content of house dust.

Mortality

Until the early 1960s the mortality from asthma was very low, about 1 per 100,000 persons annually in the age group 5–34 years. The mortality rate in

---

[1] Williams, H. and McNicol, K. N., Brit. Med. Journ., 8 November 1969.
[2] Voorhorst, R. et al. 'Allergic Asthma,' 1964, 10, 329.

England and Wales for age group 5–34 was remarkably stable during the period 1867–1961.

The number of deaths from asthma in young persons aged 5–14 years rose rapidly after 1961 to reach 76 in 1964 and 98 in 1967. In the age group 10–14 years the mortality was most marked and had increased 8-fold in 7 years. The method of treatment was studied in the case of 184 persons aged 5–34 years who died from asthma in England and Wales during the period 1966/67.[3] Two-thirds of the patients had been treated with cortico-steroids, but on investigation it was felt that it was unlikely that the use of cortico-steroids could be blamed for the rise in mortality. 84% of the patients were known to have used broncho-dilators in the form of pressurised aerosols. From evidence from other sources available to the Dunlop Committee it seemed clear that the increased mortality from asthma could be linked with the increased and probably excessive use of pressurised aerosols containing isoprenaline. In June, 1967, the Safety of Drugs Committee therefore issued a warning and arrangements were made for an injunction against excessive use to be incorporated in the instructions.

Therapy

Since 1967 when it became obvious that the numbers dying from asthma were increasing there has been a change in prescribing habits. The use of pressurised aerosols by asthmatic patients of all age groups has fallen by 20%. There is a tendency also not to use pressurised aerosols for the treatment of asthma in children. The trend now is to avoid the use of steroids in the treatment of children with asthma as, indeed, generally in the treatment of children where possible because of other effects on endocrine function. Of the newer drugs used in the treatment of asthma, 2 are of particular interest, disodium cromoglycate and salbutamol.

Disodium cromoglycate is a promising drug in the therapy of asthma in children. It appears to act by inhibiting the release of pharmacologically active amines following the antigen-antibody reaction, it also appears to inhibit the histamine hypersensitivity of bronchial smooth muscle.

Inhalations of disodium cromoglycate have been shown to inhibit the fall in vital capacity and forced expiratory volume in 1 second in patients with allergic asthma when challenged by the inhalation of appropriate antigen, and in exercise-induced asthma. No serious toxic effects have so far been reported.

Salbutamol, unlike disodium cromoglycate, is a broncho-dilator, and is probably the most important advance in bronco-dilator therapy since isoprenaline. The increasing death rate from asthma in recent years appears to be associated with the increased use or overdosage with isoprenaline. Salbutamol is a welcome introduction to therapy for whilst having the broncho-dilator effect of isoprenaline it does not have the cardiac effect. The absence of the myocardial stimulatory effect increases the safety of the drug, the broncho-dilator effect is in contrast increased, the effect lasting for $5\frac{1}{2}$ hours in the case of salbutamol compared with $1\frac{1}{2}$ hours in isoprenaline. So far the evidence suggests that salbutamol is a safer drug than isoprenaline.

---

[3] Speizer, Doll, Heaf, and Strang. Brit. Med. Journ., I, 339, 1968.

Open Air Schools

It is generally accepted that most asthmatic children improve dramatically when sent away from their homes to some form of institution caring for asthmatic children. Many authors have published evidence of remarkable improvement often without any radical change in climate.

Some local authorities in England and Wales send selected children to Davos in Switzerland. A recent paper[4] compares the results of sending 110 children from Birmingham to Davos and of admitting 60 children to Baskerville School. Of the 110 children who were treated in Switzerland 77% became symptom free during their stay, but only 13·6% remained well on return. Of the children treated in Baskerville School 66% became symptom free.

A detailed study[5] comparing the aerobiology of Davos with that of London showed that the concentration of grass pollens and other mould allergens tended to be lower in Davos. The concentration of basidiospores (from coniferous forests) was, however, much higher in Davos. It is suggested that asthmatic patients showing sensitivity to fungal spores other than Basidiomycetes are most likely to benefit from treatment in Davos.

---

[4] Morrison Smith, J., Public Health, 1970, **84**, 286.
[5] Davies, R. R., Acta Allergologica, **24**, 377, 1969.

CHAPTER VIII

THE DIABETIC CHILD

Diabetes mellitus in childhood, although fortunately a rather uncommon disease, is, nevertheless, an extremely important one. Deaf or partially hearing children are often deprived of the sympathy they deserve because their disability is not obvious either to their peers or to their elders. The diabetic child may be little less deprived than the deaf child. He grows up surrounded by adults, doctors, nurses, teachers and parents, who repeatedly assure him (and themselves) that he is a 'normal' child and can lead a 'normal' life. The partially hearing child, or children with other handicaps, are required to attend special schools or at least special classes, but the diabetic child can attend a normal class in a normal school. It is difficult for the diabetic child to understand this paradox, for he cannot live one day of his life as does any 'normal' child. He must give himself, or be given, an injection of insulin once or twice a day, every day. Meals must be assessed for carbohydrate content and the correct amount taken at the correct time. Some form of carbohydrate, such as lumps of sugar, must be carried at all times in case of emergency. When his friends suddenly decide to play games after school, the diabetic child must consider whether he requires extra carbohydrate to cover the exertion or whether it is time for the next insulin injection, besides whether he wants to play or not. These are not decisions that his 'normal' peers must consider. The child must make many such decisions and suffer many other restrictions. It is not surprising, therefore, that many diabetic children show some degree of emotional disturbance.

As the disease is uncommon in childhood, many general practitioners have no diabetic child on their list; those who do, rarely have more than one. Many schools have no diabetic pupils; those that do rarely have more than one or two. One boarding special school for children, open for 16 years, has never had a diabetic pupil, and there must be many similar schools.

It is not surprising, therefore, that although those responsible for the medical, educational or nursing care of these children will have considerable theoretical knowledge of diabetes mellitus and its control, many lack the experience of practical management of these children. The diabetic child often senses this deficiency and may in fact use it to his own ends, having days off school, missing classes he dislikes, or being excused certain activities. Confronted with a child who says he feels faint and is about to have a 'hypo' the parent or teacher cannot be blamed for becoming anxious, and responding to the child's wishes.

Fifty years ago diabetics who developed the condition in childhood died soon after, usually within 18 months of diagnosis. The introduction of insulin altered this, but to many non-medical people, the term diabetes mellitus still conjures up this picture. With this in mind it is understandable that diabetes mellitus induces varying degrees of emotional stress in parents and teachers, and this increases the likelihood that the child may become emotionally disturbed.

Nature of Diabetes

The blood sugar level in the individual is controlled by a number of factors. The most important of these is insulin. Excess of insulin results in a low blood glucose level (hypoglycaemia). Inadequate circulating glucose affects principally brain activity, leading to disturbed behaviour with loss of consciousness and even death in extreme prolonged cases. Deficiency of insulin will result in a high blood sugar (hyperglycaemia). In the diabetic subject the high blood sugar cannot be metabolized. Therefore, to meet the energy needs of the body protein is broken down, resulting in much wasting, and fat is utilised resulting in the accumulation of fatty acids and ketoacids in the blood stream. The gross metabolic disturbance, the associated acidosis and the dehydration, if uncorrected, culminate in coma and death. The diabetic child lives by negotiating the passage between a hypoglycaemic Scylla on one side and a ketoacidotic Charybdis on the other, a passage which is fortunately fairly wide and protected by warning signs and symptoms well before disaster occurs.

The manifestations of diabetes mellitus are produced by a deficiency of available effective insulin. The precise cause of the insulin deficiency or ineffectiveness is not known.

Juvenile diabetes mellitus is almost certainly multifactorial in aetiology. It has been recognised for a long time that there is a higher incidence of diabetes amongst relatives of diabetic subjects than in the general population. Much confusion exists regarding the mode of inheritance. Until quite recently the single recessive diabetic gene hypothesis was the mode of inheritance which received most support. This would mean that each parent of the diabetic child would carry the gene, and if only one parent carried the gene the child would not manifest the disease. There are, however, a number of well conducted studies which do not support this simple pattern of inheritance and the single gene hypothesis is no longer tenable. Hereditary factors probably determine the age of onset of the disease and so are of much more importance in a juvenile-onset diabetic than in the older, maturity-onset form of diabetes in which environmental factors play an increasing role. The prevalence of diabetes in siblings of the juvenile-onset diabetics compared with juvenile controls has been reported to be 25 times higher than the comparable ratio for siblings in the case of maturity-onset diabetes.

Prevalence

Between 4% and 5% of all diabetic individuals develop symptoms before the age of 15 years. In the age group 5 to 15 years the prevalence is about 1 per 1,000 school children, some authorities putting the figure a little higher and others a little lower than this. Below the age of 5 years the prevalence is much lower, falling to 0·3 per 1,000 and diabetes is very rare in the first year of life. The incidence of diabetes mellitus in children with cystic fibrosis is 10 times more common than in normal children.

65

Clinical Onset

In children the onset of diabetes is usually abrupt, the interval from the commencement of symptoms to diagnosis is on average 3 weeks. In one series of patients 10% were admitted to hospital in coma or pre-coma without prior symptoms.

The symptoms most commonly complained of are polyuria (abnormally frequent passage of urine) and polydipsia (excessive drinking), and are present in almost 90% of patients. Weight loss and excessive appetite are the next most frequently noted symptoms and occur in about 50% of cases. In just over 30% of patients the onset of symptoms is associated with infection. Severe emotional trauma has frequently been associated with the onset of symptoms.

The physical state of the child at the time of diagnosis varies considerably. The parent may bring the child to the doctor complaining of polyuria, polydipsia and weight loss. The child may not be particularly ill at this stage or he or she may be much more ill than his or her appearance would suggest. Alternatively, the child may be acutely ill; about one fifth of all cases are admitted to hospital in coma or pre-coma. There has usually been a period of polyuria and polydipsia followed by vomiting, abdominal pain and dehydration; the symptoms become rapidly worse until emergency admission to hospital is inevitable. Diabetic pre-coma, or coma, is a medical emergency with a substantial rate of death.

Therapy

Following confirmation of the diagnosis and correction of the acute metabolic disturbance in hospital involving fluid and electrolyte replacement, insulin administration and treatment of infection, the important stage of stabilisation of the diabetes and education of the child and parents begins. Diabetes starting in childhood almost invariably will require the life-long administration of insulin by injection for control of the disease. There is a wide variety of insulin preparations; soluble insulin is the standby for treatment of emergencies for it acts quickly and lasts for only 4 to 8 hours. Other preparations of insulin vary in having longer periods of action. Soluble insulin must be given at least twice a day for adequate long-term control. Although the long-acting insulin may only need to be given once per day many diabetologists regard twice daily soluble insulin as the treatment of choice in the control of diabetes in children.

In the insulin-dependent juvenile-onset patient, carbohydrate intake *regulation* is sought, an adequate and stable daily total being allowed, properly spaced through the day to fit the insulin requirement for the natural rhythms of activity and rest. For the maturity-onset patient, carbohydrate (and, in the obese, total calorie) *restriction* is the guiding principle in recommending diet. This difference between *regulation* and *restriction* should be clearly understood and no diabetic child need be deprived of adequate carbohydrate.

Although very young children may appear able to look after themselves, it has been shown that they may fail fully to appreciate the significance of urine testing, diet and the necessity of regular injections until the age of 10 or 12 years.

Hypoglycaemia

If inadequate carbohydrate is taken or too much insulin is given, the blood sugar will drop below the normal range. The parents and teachers must be able to recognise these insulin 'reactions' in their early stages. The treatment at an early stage is simply one of giving rapidly absorbable carbohydrate such as sugar and glucose tablets. Teachers with a diabetic child in their class will find it desirable to keep a small supply of carbohydrates such as glucose sweets handy. If consciousness is lost, intravenous glucose solution or glucagon injection may be required but that, of course, would be for action outside the school health service.

Dental Care

Regular dental inspection and care are important for the diabetic child, as for all children.

School

With proper management the diabetic child can and should be educated at an ordinary school. There are, however, some diabetic children who, because of difficulty in controlling their diabetes, social factors, or emotional problems, require special schooling. The diabetic child will benefit immensely from periods spent with other diabetic children. Holidays spent at one of the children's camps organised by the British Diabetic Association will help the child realise that other children have similar problems to himself and foster a spirit of self-confidence and independence. Children whose diabetes is difficult to control frequently respond very quickly when living with other diabetic children in a special school. An outstanding example of how a diabetic child should be educated and how they can learn to master their handicap is seen in children attending Palingswick House in London. Parents of diabetic children can get much help from membership of the British Diabetic Association and should be encouraged to join. Special discussion groups for parents and a wealth of printed material are provided by the Association (3–6 Alfred Place, London WC1).

Prognosis

Although the immediate prognosis in diabetes has dramatically improved, the incidence of long term complications is still depressing. In one series, when the total duration of the disease was 15 years or more, 80% had a retinopathy or vascular disease and 40% had disease of the kidney. In another series, when the disease was of 20 years' duration, 82% had retinopathy, 73% had vascular disease and 41% kidney disease. The mortality in both series was high. The average expectation of life is less than 20 years from diagnosis and death in the young is more likely to be due to the microvascular complications than the metabolic disorder itself. Diabetic boys tend to be shorter and to weigh less than controls. Diabetic children are absent from school for longer periods than non-diabetic children.

An adverse effect of diabetes on intelligence of the child is very doubtful. In one small series where diabetes started before the age of 5 years, the child's I.Q. was significantly lower than that of his non-diabetic siblings.

Emotional Problems

As indicated in the introduction, in view of the overall effect of diabetes on the life of the child and the parents, it is not surprising that emotional difficulties are common in diabetic children. It has been shown that, as might be expected, anxiety symptoms are more prominent in mothers of diabetic children than in mothers of normal children.

The only solution to this problem is for parents and anyone with responsibility for the child, such as teachers, to have a sound understanding of the disease and its management.

CHAPTER IX

VISUALLY HANDICAPPED CHILDREN

The size of this problem

Variations in eyesight were, as usual, the commonest condition recorded in the medical examination of school children. Of the 3 million seen out of the 8 million school population in 1969, approximately 145,000 required treatment and another 145,000 observation for refractive variations; a further 22,000 required treatment for squint with 20,000 placed under observation for this condition. In all, 404,000 children were treated either by members of local education authority staff or in school eye clinics by regional hospital board staff, or were known to have been treated elsewhere during the year, and, of these, 202,000 were prescribed spectacles.

Vision testing in schools

Short courses of training for medical officers in the detection and management of visual abnormalities in children have continued in various parts of the country and have been well supported. The testing material for young children has recently been supplemented by the introduction of Ffook's symbols which are supplied in either card or cube form for the tester, with matching cut out symbols used by the child.

During 1969, screening of visual acuity for distance was carried out during the first year at school by 150 of the 163 local education authorities, while 6 delayed for one year and 7 for two years.

Annual review was achieved in 21 areas; many other L.E.A.s carried out tests in alternate years or less frequently. One local education authority, however, did no screening of vision after the age of 8 and another continued testing at 7 and 14 years of age, with annual review, however, only of those already wearing spectacles. Whenever screening is delayed, it is followed by an unusually large crop of referrals at the next examination. Some of these children will have needed glasses or other help for a considerable time before being identified, and their education and general welfare may have suffered unnecessarily during the interim period. The value of regular and frequent testing of visual acuity by skilled and reliable staff is a rewarding contribution to the health of the school child.

Screening was carried out by a variety of staff, ranging from clerks, education welfare officers, and audiometricians to school nurses, health visitors and school medical officers; in one small and isolated region an optician was employed. Use of vision-screening machines followed no pattern, although it is thought not to be the method of choice for children in infant schools. The school doctor or health visitor reassesses any failures from screening machines to prevent unnecessary referral of children to ophthalmologists. Children should of course be referred as soon as they are suspected of having squints; in at least one area an orthoptist screens all children in nursery schools, day nurseries and all entrants to infant schools for latent squint.

Colour Vision

Colour vision testing using Ishihara plates was carried out in all but 8 areas, but in 42 of these was for boys only. The age of testing varied from 5 to 15, but did not necessarily coincide with the assessment of visual acuity. For young children unfamiliar with numbers in whom a learning difficulty associated with the use of colour has to be excluded, an adaptation using coloured symbols and matching shapes has been devised by Gardiner, but is not yet available commercially.

Few ophthalmologists carry out further investigation of abnormal colour vision so long as the visual acuity is normal, but[1] Sarwar has made a series of observations on Oxford school children referred to him. Using Ishihara test plates and the Giles Archer lantern, he found improvement in colour perception in a high proportion of children carrying out daily exercises with blue, green and red filters for several weeks or months.

Committee of Enquiry into the Education of Visually Handicapped Children

The interest of school medical officers and others concerned with children's vision has been sustained by the deliberations of the Committee of Enquiry into the Education of Visually Handicapped Children, whose report is expected later this year. Particular attention has been paid to the needs of the young child suspected or found to have a significant visual abnormality, and the importance of teamwork by the various disciplines has been stressed, so that the maximum amount of meaningful help can be given to the parents as early as possible. Evidence submitted to the Committee as 'Notes for parents in the management of visually impaired children at home' has been circulated to principal school medical officers for distribution to doctors and health visitors and was enthusiastically welcomed as useful information towards remedying a regrettable deficiency. Consideration is being given to the alternative ways of educating blind and partially sighted children at different stages of their school careers and to the medical requirements from ophthalmologists, paediatricians, and other specialists as well as for their general medical care and supervision.

Not enough is known about children with significant visual difficulties in ordinary schools and in schools for children with other handicaps. No information is available of the numbers of children for whom glasses are prescribed but who, for one reason or another, especially breakages and repairs, have to function for much of the time without them and so are working with impaired vision. Unfortunately, it is all too rare for a child, even in a school for the visually handicapped, to have an efficient spare pair of glasses, and outgrown frames and lenses are all too often brought back into use.

A survey was carried out in 1969–70 in Cheshire, Birkenhead, Chester, Stockport, and Wallasey of children in ordinary schools and in special schools other than those for the blind or the partially sighted with visual acuity of 6/18 or less in the better eye, even with glasses. Compared with a total of

---

[1] Annals of Ophthalmology, September 1970, pp. 582–587.

68 children receiving special educational treatment as partially sighted pupils, there were 54 in ordinary schools of whom 7 had additional handicaps. Extra help was available for 12 of the children, including 5 in one area visited by a peripatetic teacher of the visually handicapped. There were 7 children known to have poor visual acuity in other special schools. In a survey in Wales during 1969–70, 78 children with significant visual defects were identified in the ordinary schools compared with 110 in schools for partially sighted pupils. Of the 78, 46 were being observed, 13 were on the waiting list for special school, the parents of 16 children had refused special school placement and details for 3 were not available.

The national incidence of blind children per 10,000 school population in 1969 was 1·66 compared with 2·93 for partially sighted children. There were wide variations in ascertainment rates throughout England and Wales, those for the partially sighted being particularly high in Greater London and the Midlands, and in areas where day special educational treatment was available. All this suggests that there are still many children in ordinary schools who could benefit from additional help because of their defective vision.

CHAPTER X

SURVEY OF 15-YEAR-OLD PUPILS IN SCHOOLS FOR THE DEAF, 1969–70

A survey of 15-year-old pupils in schools for the deaf was carried out by one of the Department's medical officers in 1962–63 and reported on in 'The Health of the School Child 1962–63'. At the end of this report the intention was declared to carry out a similar survey in about 5 years' time, but in the event seven years passed before another survey was possible. It was carried out by the same medical officer during 1969/1970 and the opportunity was taken when arranging it to ask head teachers for their comments on the earlier one. Several head teachers suggested that social handicap could be an important factor in the success or otherwise of deaf pupils, so that in the current survey an attempt was made to include this among the additional handicaps recorded. There was also some criticism of the weight given in the previous survey to the children's intelligence quotients as assessed on the performance scale of the Wechsler Intelligence Scale for Children. It was pointed out, quite rightly, that many deaf children are now subjected to the Wechsler Performance Test so often by research workers of various kinds that children have been observed to be able to perform some of the tests without reference to the instructions. The earlier report commented on the number of children with high scores on a performance test who failed at the interview stage for admission to the selective schools for deaf children. It was pointed out by a very experienced and able headmaster that for an academic education both verbal ability and verbal attainments are absolutely essential. In the current survey, therefore, although performance I.Q.s were available for most of the children included in the survey, the results will not be included in the report other than by including some of them in the category of educationally subnormal in the list of additional handicaps.

A combination of circumstances led to it being impossible for the medical officer concerned to visit all schools in the time available. Thirty-five schools were approached to seek their co-operation in a survey of children born in 1954. Five schools had no pupils in this age group; of the remaining 30 schools the medical officer visited 20 (10 day and 10 boarding) schools and interviewed 167 children, comprising 91 boys and 76 girls. Thirty-five of the boys and 27 of the girls were day pupils, 56 boys and 49 girls were boarders. From the other 10 schools head teachers very kindly completed pro formata for 51 children making a total of 218 in the age range surveyed. This compares with a total of 359 in the previous survey and reflects the change in pattern of educational provision for some children with hearing impairment. During the period of the survey 32 children in the age group left school before being interviewed and at the time this report was completed all but four of them were satisfactorily placed in employment.

72

Hearing Loss

All the children surveyed had a bilateral hearing loss. As in the earlier survey the loss for speech in the better ear was assumed to be related to the average loss at the three frequencies: 500, 1,000 and 2,000 cycles per second. Table I shows the distribution and gives the comparative incidence in the previous survey.

TABLE I

Decibels	Boys	Girls	Total	% 1969–1970	% 1962–1963
Less than 60 ..	13	11	24	14·3	7·7
61–70 ..	15	10	25	14·9	15·3
71–80 ..	16	12	28	16·8	14·9
81–90 ..	20	19	39	23·4	24·2
91–100 ..	14	13	27	16·2	21·2
101–110 ..	7	5	12	7·2	5·3
111 and over..	6	6	12	7·2	11·4
Total ..	91	76	167	100·0	100·0

It was somewhat surprising to find more children with a hearing loss for pure tones of less than 60 decibels in the schools for the deaf in 1969 than in 1962, in view of the development of additional special educational provision for hearing impaired children in special units and classes. It must be pointed out, however, that some of these children who appeared to have much useful residual hearing had had a trial in one of these classes and had failed to make satisfactory progress. In addition, a number of them had handicaps additional to the hearing impairment.

Causes of Deafness

Compared with 7 years ago, the reported cases of deafness showed a marked reduction in the relative incidence of infective conditions—from 24·5 per cent in 1962/63 to 7·8 per cent in 1969/70 reflecting the further developments in treatment of such conditions. There was a marked increase, however, in deafness considered to be due to perinatal conditions, including rhesus incompatibility and other causes of severe jaundice, prematurity, anoxia and birth injury. From

TABLE II

Summary of causes

	Boys	Girls	Total	% 1969–70	% 1962–63
Born deaf	29	21	50 ⎱ 80	29·9 ⎱ 47·9	49·2 ⎱ 60·6
Born deaf into deaf family	15	15	30 ⎰	18·0 ⎰	11·4 ⎰
Perinatal causes ..	16	11	27	16·2	1·4
Infections	5	8	13	7·8	24·5
Mixed conductive and perceptive	7	2	9	5·3	3·1
Conductive	1	4	5	3·0	—
Trauma	—	3	3	1·8	0·6
Maternal Rubella ..	1	1	2	1·2	2·8
Unknown	17	11	28	16·8	7·0
Total	91	76	167	100·0	100·0

73

1·4 per cent, due to kernicterus in 1962/63, the incidence has risen to 16·2 per cent due to perinatal causes, including kernicterus in the current survey. This increase reflects the increased survival rate of these babies.

Additional Handicaps

As stated earlier, it was decided to include social problems in the list of additional handicaps. More than one head teacher referred to the importance of this and mentioned a significant variability in the audiograms of some children with emotional problems arising from disturbances in the stability of the home situation. For example, divorced or estranged parents, frequent moves of home, jealousy of and rivalry between brothers and sisters. The cause of this variability may be due to an attention factor with a possible limiting effect upon the development of speech, lip-reading and general educational attainment. Failure in attention of this kind is even more important to a child with hearing impairment than to one with normal hearing since the effort to follow speech on a speaker's lips and coincidentally to interpret amplified (and sometimes distorted-sound, has to be concentrated and continuous. The hearing impaired child cannot afford to lose even the smallest link in the communication chain. Ninety-nine additional handicaps of significant severity were found in 91 of the 167 children. These are tabulated below.

TABLE III

Additional handicaps

Handicap	Boys	Girls	Total	% 1969–70	% 1962–63
Vision	13	12	25	15·0	18·1
Social problems ..	11	12	23	13·8	—
Maladjustment ..	15	7	22	13·2	11·7
Educational subnormality	6	4	10	6·0	—
Physical handicap ..	4	6	10	5·9	7·6
Non-English speaking family	3	3	6	3·6	2·8
Late entrant	3	—	3	1·8	5·3
Total	55	44	99	59·3	45·5

Ability to Communicate by Speech

All 167 children were interviewed individually to assess their ability to communicate with a stranger, either orally or by other means. As in the previous survey three broad groups were defined: those with clear, intelligible speech and good lip-reading ability with whom communication was easy, at least for the interviewer; those who had unintelligible speech and varying degrees of difficulty in lip-reading or otherwise understanding the interviewer; and those

TABLE IV

	Boys	Girls	Total	% 1969–70	% 1962–63
Intelligible speech ..	29	36	65	38·9	22·3
Partly intelligible speech	44	31	75	44·9	54·7
No intelligible speech ..	18	9	27	16·2	23·0

74

in between, who had less than easily intelligible speech and who sometimes needed other than oral clues to help them. This generally meant writing as the interviewer was unable either to finger-spell or sign. The distribution of speech intelligibility is shown in Table IV.

Children with Good Intelligible Speech

There were 65 of these, 29 boys and 36 girls, 24 of them being in day schools and 41 in boarding schools. This gives an incidence of 38·9% of all children in the survey compared with 22·3% in the earlier survey.

The distribution of hearing loss, causes and additional handicaps among these 65 children is shown in Tables V, VI and VII. It may be of interest that 24 of these children come from two selective secondary schools and were therefore boarders. Of the remaining 41 children, 18 were boarders and 23 were day pupils coming from 14 out of the 20 schools visited.

TABLE V
Hearing loss

Decibels	Boys	Girls	Total	% 1969–70	% 1962–63
Less than 60	9	9	18	27·7	26·2
61–70	6	6	12	18·5	26·2
71–80	3	6	9	13·8	20·0
81–90	6	8	14	21·5	15·0
91–100	3	5	8	12·3	8·8
101–110	2	2	4	6·2	3·8
Total	29	36	65	100·0	100·0

TABLE VI
Causes of deafness

	Boys	Girls	Total	% 1969–70	% 1962–63
Born deaf	10	11	21	32·2	43·7
Born deaf into deaf family	4	8	12	18·5	17·5
Perinatal	4	7	11	16·9	—
Infection	2	2	4	6·2	20·0
Mixed conductive and perceptive	3	1	4	6·2	6·3
Conductive	1	3	4	6·2	—
Trauma	—	1	1	1·5	—
Unknown	5	3	8	12·3	10·0
Total	29	36	65	100·0	97·5

TABLE VII
Additional handicaps

Handicap	Boys	Girls	Total	% 1969–70	% 1962–63
Vision	5	5	10	15·4	22·5
Social problem	5	3	8	12·3	—
Maladjustment	4	3	7	10·8	—
Physical handicap	2	3	5	7·7	1·25
Non-English Speaking	1	1	2	3·0	1·25
Total	17	15	32	49·2	25·00

In this group of 65 children the 32 additional handicaps were shared among 29 children, fewer than half of the group. In other words, more than half of the children had, as far as one could discover, only a hearing impairment to contend with. By contrast it will be shown in a subsequent table that only about 7% of children in the speechless group had no additional handicap. None of the 10 children thought to be educationally subnormal appears in the group with intelligible speech even though some of these children had much useful residual hearing.

Children with Partly Intelligible Speech

There were 75 of these and details of hearing loss, causes of deafness and incidence of additional handicaps are shown in Tables VIII, IX and X.

TABLE VIII

Hearing loss

Decibels	Boys	Girls	Total	% 1969–70	% 1962–63
60	4	2	6	8·00	3·5
61–70	8	4	12	16·00	15·8
71–80	10	4	14	18·70	15·8
81–90	9	9	18	24·00	23·5
91–100	7	6	13	17·30	24·6
101–110	3	3	6	8·00	6·6
111 and over ..	3	3	6	8·00	10·2
Total	44	31	75	100·00	100·00

TABLE IX

Causes

	Boys	Girls	Total	% 1969–70	% 1962–63
Born deaf	9	6	15	20·0	52·1
Born deaf into deaf family	8	5	13	17·4	7·7
Perinatal	12	4	16	21·3	2·5
Infections	2	5	7	9·3	25·0
Mixed conductive and perceptive	2	1	3	4·0	2·5
Conductive	—	1	1	1·3	—
Trauma	—	2	2	2·7	1·0
Maternal rubella ..	1	1	2	2·7	3·1
Unknown	10	6	16	21·3	6·1
Total	44	31	75	100·0	100·0

TABLE X

Additional handicap

	Boys	Girls	Total	% 1969–70	% 1962–63
Social	4	6	10	13·3	—
Vision	4	5	9	12·0	17·9
Maladjustment ..	6	3	9	12·0	15·3
Educationally Subnormal	3	2	5	6·65	—
Physical handicap ..	2	3	5	6·65	7·7
Late entrant	2	—	2	2·7	—
Non-English speaking	1	1	2	2·7	2·0
Total	22	20	42	56·00	42·9

Children with no Intelligible Speech

Twenty-seven of the 167 children (16%) had no speech that was intelligible to a stranger though, as in the previous survey, teachers more familiar with the children's patterns of utterance were often able to interpret correctly. Seventeen of these children were boarders, 10 were day pupils, and they were attending 12 of the 20 schools visited. Three of these children made no attempt to lip-read but obviously preferred manual communication and expected this form of communication to be understood. The degree to which communication was possible, even without speech on the part of the child, was extremely variable. Some children were good lip-readers and used writing to maintain communication. Others expected their 'speech' to be understood or the interviewer to understand manual communication. Some did not seem to try to keep any sort of communication going and with the enormous difficulties faced by these children it is not surprising that some of them give up the unequal struggle.

The hearing loss, causes of deafness and incidence of additional handicaps in this group are tabulated below.

TABLE XI

Hearing loss

Decibels	Boys	Girls	Total	% 1969–70	% 1962–63
61–70	1	—	1	3·7	3·6
71–80	3	2	5	18·5	7·3
81–90	5	2	7	25·9	35·0
91–100	4	2	6	22·3	25·2
101–110	2	—	2	7·4	7·3
111 and over	3	3	6	22·2	21·6
Total	18	9	27	100·0	100·0

TABLE XII

Causes

	Boys	Girls	Total	% 1969–70	% 1962–63
Born deaf	10	4	14	51·9	48·2
Born into deaf family	3	2	5	18·5	14·5
Infection	1	1	2	7·4	27·7
Mixed	2	—	2	7·4	1·2
Rubella (maternal)	—	—	—	—	2·4
Unknown	2	2	4	14·8	6·0
Total	18	9	27	100·0	100·0

TABLE XIII

Additional handicap

	Boys	Girls	Total	% 1969–70	% 1962–63
Vision	4	2	6	22·3	14·5
Maladjustment	5	1	6	22·3	14·5
Social problems	2	3	5	18·5	—
Educationally subnormal	3	2	5	18·5	38·5
Non-English Speaking	1	1	2	7·4	6·0
Late entrant	1	—	1	3·7	15·7
Total	16	9	25	92·7	89·2

The teachers' assessment of the 51 children not seen by the Department's medical officer produced the following assessment as far as speech intelligibility is concerned:

Good intelligible speech	Partly intelligible speech	No intelligible speech
31·4%	47·0%	21·6%

This, at first sight, does not seem to relate very closely to the medical officer's findings among the 167 children. If, however, the number of grammar school pupils is subtracted from the medical officer's figures the following results are obtained:

Good intelligible speech	Partly intelligible speech	No intelligible speech
32·4%	46·4%	21·2%

These findings were encouraging to the medical officer concerned in so far as they seemed to suggest that her assessments were not so different from those made by teachers, although the size of the sample was different.

Conclusion

The many possible variations in the cause of hearing impairment and of combinations of additional handicap as well as changes in educational provision mean that it is impossible to compare directly a group of handicapped pupils with those of similar age several years later. What the survey does show, however, is that, as in the previous one, a significant proportion of children leave schools for the deaf with speech unintelligible to a stranger and with all that this failure of two-way communication implies. Some of these children are good lip-readers and can understand the speech of others but are unable to reply in the way expected by the public generally. This then may lead to the misunderstandings which so often add to the already considerable difficulties faced by the adolescent with a hearing impairment in finding suitable employment and fitting in to the speaking and hearing community.

CHAPTER XI

DISEASES OF THE SKIN

In recent years there has been an increase in the numbers of school children reported with ringworm, scabies and impetigo; there has been a decrease, noted in 1969 and continuing in 1970, in those reported with impetigo. The number of school children reported as having other skin diseases remains unchanged. Although many of these skin diseases are relatively minor, they are often troublesome and may be the cause of prolonged absence from school.

Verminous Conditions

The frequency of verminous conditions in children attending school, had been slowly falling, but a moderate increase in the number and rate per 100,000 pupils was noted in 1969; a more marked increase in verminous infestation was reported by principal school medical officers in 1970.

The table, given below, shows the number of school children found to be infested and the rate per 100,000 during the 6 year period 1965–70, reported by school health departments. These numbers are still disturbingly large.

TABLE I

Year	Number infested	School population	Rate per 100,000 School children
1965	177,871	6·826 million	2,605·1
1966	176,960	6·982 million	2,534·4
1967	182,798	7·167 million	2,550·2
1968	172,384	7·372 million	2,338·1
1969	192,896	7·592 million	2,504·6
1970	223,422	7·717 million	2,895.0

In 1969, 29,852 cleansing notices were issued, this being almost the same number as in 1965 (29,583): cleansing orders issued in 1969 totalled 6,473 as compared to 7,002 in 1965.

These figures are disappointing, and will give little comfort or encouragement to school nurses and cleansing assistants on whose time and energy these verminous conditions continue to make heavy demands. Although many of these children may only have slight infestations, it remains essential, if these conditions are to be eradicated from the school population to maintain regular inspections for cleanliness and to follow up those children found to be verminous.

It would seem likely that the figures quoted above, of children infested with vermin, are underestimated. For example, older children who are thought to be capable of maintaining their personal hygiene may not be regularly inspected to ensure freedom from infestation: minimal degrees of infestation with nits may not be recorded: nor do these figures include those children in the former junior training centres.

An interesting survey of verminous infestation among school children is reported by the Principal School Medical Officer of Teesside (1) in which a stratified sample from infant and junior schools were inspected on the second day of the Autumn term 1970. This sample comprised 3,576 pupils, of whom 1 in 7 children (15·8%) were found to have some degree of infestation. The findings in relation to 600 senior pupils from 2 secondary schools examined on the same day, showed that 1 in 4 (26·5%) was infested to some degree. Thirty of the 159 senior pupils infested were in the 14–15 year group and might have been expected, given reasonable home conditions, to be able to keep themselves clean. These findings were considered to be so significant that the authority has launched a vigorous campaign, including local press coverage, to deal with the problem of head infestation within the authority. This campaign has been successful in reducing the incidence of infestation in Teesside school children, and in reminding parents of the need to keep their children free from vermin.[1]

It is uncertain to what extent the present trend for the wearing of long hair by adolescents, many of whom are remaining longer at school, may have contributed to the present unsatisfactory position regarding verminous infestation. Infestation in senior boys used to be uncommon, but with long hair now popular among both sexes and the habit of boys and girls walking along with arms entwined around each other's necks, spread of infestation is to be expected. Certainly long hair will require greater precaution against infestation.

Verminous infestation is basically a family problem and to eradicate it the whole family must become clean. The school nurse and her assistant have a major part to play in the health education of children and parents by encouraging personal hygiene and care of the hair, and in the use of modern insecticides which are now available.

Evidence of resistance by head and body lice to DDT and dieldrin insecticides appears to be accumulating: Maunder[2] reporting the results of a survey among London school children, observed that head lice now tolerated doses of organochlorine insecticides well in excess of lethal dosages of 20 years ago when these insecticides were first used. Resistant strains of head lice have been suspected in several areas, and have been observed in a residential school, where the infestation only responded to prolonged attention to personal hygiene and fine-tooth combing of the hair.

Among newer insecticides, Maunder suggests that Malathion and Carbaryl preparations may be advantageous. Malathion has an ovicidal action as well as killing the louse; Carbaryl has an extremely fast action against head lice.

Impetigo

Impetigo has been reported with increasing frequency in children of school age in recent years; the number reported in 1969 (9,468), however, shows a decrease of slightly over 1,000 cases over the figures reported for 1968. The number of school children suffering from impetigo in 1970 (8,505) shows a continuation

---

[1] Principal School Medical Officer, Report, Teesside G.B.
[2] Maunder, J. W. Medical Officer: 8.1.71, pp. 27–29.

of this downward trend. Nevertheless, despite the reduction in the incidence of the disease, the numbers of school children suffering from impetigo remains unsatisfactory.

This contagious skin infection is caused by staphylococci or streptococci which may be spread in a variety of ways from other septic lesions, by direct or indirect contact with other infected persons, or as a secondary complication of other skin conditions such as scabies, ringworm or verminous infestation.

It is characterized by the development of thin walled vesicles and bullae which are ruptured by the scratching of this itchy lesion; scratching also leads to spread of the lesion to other parts. The most frequently affected areas are the face and ears, and the condition is most commonly seen in children. Individual lesions vary in size and are usually circular in appearance. If untreated the lesions often tend to heal spontaneously in 4–6 weeks.

Treatment is by giving an antibiotic ointment to which the causative organism is sensitive; this should be applied twice daily and the lesions covered. Application of fluorinated cortico-steroids should be avoided, as these interfere with the natural resistance of the skin to the infection. Indiscriminate use of these on all types of skin disease, including impetigo and ringworm, may be partly responsible for prolonging the infection and thereby increasing the chances of its spreading to others.

Recovery usually takes place in 7–10 days; impetigo should not normally be a reason for prolonged absence from school. Attention should be paid to strict personal hygiene and to possible sources of infection in the nose and ears.

Scabies

Scabies is an inflammation of the skin caused by a mite infestation with Sarcoptes Scabiei (hominis). The irritation of the skin, caused by the presence of the itch mite, leads to scratching and secondary infection. The disease is normally contracted from other infected persons, but rarely may be contracted from domestic animals.

The incidence of the disease has increased markedly in recent years in school children in England. Table II shows that there has been almost a fourfold increase in scabies in the period 1965–70.

TABLE II

Year	Number treated	School population	Incidence per 100,000 pupils
1965	4,446	6,826,400	68·1
1966	6,180	6,982,191	97·5
1967	10,945	7,167,984	152·7
1968	13,837	7,372,847	187·7
1969	17,282	7,592,674	227·6
1970	17,275	7,717,179	223·8

While there has been an overall increase in the incidence of scabies throughout England, regional variations have been most evident in Eastern and Midland regions and in the East and West Riding of Yorkshire. In these regions the numbers of school children being treated increased sixfold between 1965 and

81

1969; although these 3 regions have reported decreases in incidence in 1970, the numbers of infested school children remains disturbingly high (Table III). There would appear to be no firm evidence that the spread of the disease is abating: in 1970, this upward trend continued particularly in Northern, North Western and Metropolitan regions (Table IV).

TABLE III

Region	1965	1966	1967	1968	1969	1970
Eastern	29	120	108	226	181	173
Midland	722	1,199	3,185	4,449	4,914	4,461
Yorks: E. and W. Riding ..	523	847	1,376	2,297	3,121	2,825

TABLE IV

Region	1965	1966	1967	1968	1969	1970
Northern	686	1,007	1,357	1,181	2,142	2,400
North Western	1,462	2,034	2,704	2,941	3,663	3,935
Metropolitan	616	1,000	1,234	1,433	1,919	2,124

The mite causing scabies is a minute parasite; the female is larger than the male and is just visible to the naked eye. The female burrows into the horny epidermis and lays eggs as she progresses. The lifespan of the female is about 8 weeks, during which time she will lay about 50 eggs which will hatch out after 3 days, producing six-legged larvae. These larvae migrate to other parts of the skin, and cause irritation once the individual has become sensitised to the mite. The larva moults within 2 or 3 days after which it changes into an eight-legged nymph, which after another 2 or 3 days becomes an adult mite.

After fertilisation the female enlarges and burrows into the horny dermis. The parasite usually burrows into specific areas of the skin (e.g. interdigital skin, anterior aspect of wrist, ulnar aspect of palms and forearms, elbow region, anterior axilla, peri-umbilicus and buttocks; the face is rarely affected). The most common sites of burrowing are the hands and wrists.

Symptoms do not appear for several weeks after first infestation by the parasite; the irritation caused by the mite being due to the sensitisation reaction of the patient to the parasite. The rash of scabies may be either a thin sinuous burrow, from a half to one centimetre long; or a papular rash (caused by immature forms in hair follicles, or by non-specific urticarial reaction from sensitisation by the adult parasite). Secondary infection from scratching is common and gives rise to weeping or crusted lesions of the skin. Dermatitis herpetiformis, pediculosis or papular urticaria ('heat spots') may be confused with scabies.

Dermatitis herpetiformis is relatively rare and occurs mainly in adults, producing small itching vesicles, the distribution of these lesions being different from scabies. The eruption of pediculosis corporis is unlike that of scabies in distribution and appearance, and lice may be found in the seams of the under-clothing. Papular urticaria differs from scabies in that the distribution of the rash tends to be symmetrical affecting lower limbs, buttocks and forearms. The lesions consist of small, intensely itchy papules which easily become secondarily infected by scratching.

Transmission of scabies, from one person to another, is by close contact with an infected person. It is important to note that symptoms may not be manifest for some 4 or 5 weeks after the original infection and all known contacts of a case of scabies should be examined to control the spread of the disease. Scabies is commonly a household infection and home contacts must always be suspect.

Treatment of scabies should be intensive. The skin of the patient should be treated from the neck to the soles of the feet, and all contacts should be treated at the same time. Benzyl Benzoate BP is commonly used in treating the condition: Lorexane (1% gamma benzene hexachloride), Tetmosol (25% monosulphiram diluted with 3 parts of water just before use), and Eurax (Crotonuton) are newer and less irritating preparations. The routine for treatment of scabies should be:[3]

1. A hot bath using soap and gentle rubbing with a flannel particularly in areas of burrowing.
2. Drying with a towel.
3. Application of the preparation on the whole body from chin to soles of feet; the preparation should be allowed to dry on the skin.
4. Patient goes to bed; the preparation on the skin will kill any mites in the bedclothes.
5. The application of the preparation is repeated next day; bathing is not required.
6. The preparation is washed off by bathing on the third day.

Continuation of the symptoms after a fortnight indicates a reinfection or inadequate treatment. The routine given above should be repeated and an intensive search made for untreated contacts.

Scabies is rarely contracted from clothing or bedding; disinfestation is, therefore, unnecessary.

Ringworm

Since 1965 there has been an increase in the number of children reported with ringworm of both scalp and body in England: in 1970, the number of scalp infections doubled, while body infections decreased by about one-fifth.

Regional variations occur; the South Western region of England, which recorded high rates in the early part of the 6-year-period 1965/70, has since

TABLE V

Year	Number of scalp infections	Number of body infections	Total
1965	181	597	778
1966	175	610	765
1967	287	572	859
1968	411	724	1,135
1969	429	722	1,151
1970	891	584	1,475

[3] Scabies: DHSS, December 1970.

shown a gradual decrease. Conversely North Midlands and Midland regions particularly, have recorded steady increases since 1967. The steadily increasing incidence in total number of infections shows no evidence that the condition is abating.

Ringworm may affect the skin (Tinea corporis), nails (Tinea unguium) or scalp (Tinea capitis). The condition is due to a superficial infection of the skin by a fungus which digests keratin in the dead horny layer; living tissue is rarely involved. The genera of fungi involved are Trichophyton, Microsporon and Epidermophyton. Ringworm is neither very infectious nor contagious; individual susceptibility and hyperhydrosis are predisposing factors in contracting the disease.

The diagnosis of ringworm may be confirmed by microscopic examination of scrapings from the infected skin placed in 10% Potassium Hydroxide. Confirmation of the diagnosis may be obtained by culturing the fungus which may be used in identifying the species involved.

Wood's light may be helpful in detecting ringworm of the scalp in children. It is only of value in detecting small spored ringworm (Microsporon canis and Microsporon audouini) when the infected hairs fluoresce with a greenish colour. It will not detect the Trichophyton infections of the scalp common among immigrants.

Tinea corporis (ringworm of the body) may be caused by several species of trichophyton or microsporon and children are more commonly infected than adults.

The lesions may be:

1. Annular: producing a ring of red lesions with a central scaly area; the scalp may also be affected.
2. Follicular: producing a pustular folliculitis affecting neck, shoulder and arm regions; the folliculitis may become granulomatous. This follicular type is sometimes associated with animal vectors e.g. cats, dogs or pet mice.
3. Plaque: these are disc-like lesions which appear less inflamed than the annular type; the scalp may also be involved.
4. Granulomatous: these lesions may resemble carbuncles.

Tinea cruris (ringworm of the groin: Dhobi itch) occurs mainly in males and is seen from time to time in adolescent schoolboys. It produces an annular type of lesion in the groin which is asymmetrical, bilateral and often intensely itchy. Treatment by a topical fungicidal ointment is effective; griseofulvin is the drug of choice in resistant cases.

Tinea capitis (ringworm of the scalp) occurs most frequently in children below the age of puberty. The lesions consist of scaly patches, of varying sizes, in which fragmented hairs may be seen. The onset of these lesions is gradual and if untreated may spread to eyelids, neck or trunk being involved; these areas should be examined to preclude spread of the lesions. Griseofulvin is the drug of choice, with local application of a fungicidal ointment.

Tinea unguium (ringworm of the nails) is invariably associated with ringworm of the feet (Tinea pedis). The affected nails may show varying degrees of deformity from virtually no to almost total disintegration. Griseofulvin medication over a period of many months may be required to effect a cure of this condition. Tinea pedis (ringworm of the feet) occurs commonly in young and middle aged males and rarely in children; it is frequently seen in adolescent youths in school. It may be acute or chronic in type. The acute variety begins with the sudden appearance of an acute itchy vesicular eruption in the clefts between the toes; this may spread over the feet and legs. The chronic type is a mild infection involving toes, soles, heels and sides of the feet (moccasin type).

Griseofulvin

Griseofulvin is an antibiotic obtained from several species of penicillium; it was introduced into the treatment of superficial fungal diseases in 1959 and is effective against Trichophyton, Epidermophyton and Microsporon strains. It is in-effective against Candida albicans (Monilia) and Microsporon furfur (Pityriasis versicolor). Resistance to the drug is rare and side effects (headache, diarrhoea, nausea, vomiting, urticaria and sunlight sensitivity) are very uncommon. The adult dose is 0·5 g of fine particle Griseofulvin and the dose for a child is correspondingly lower, but since the drug is fungistatic and not fungicidal, it must be given in an adequate dosage daily to ensure that the concentration in the keratin is sufficient to stop invasion of the impregnated keratin by the fungus. As the keratin is shed, the fungus is eliminated, but it follows that the drug must be taken until all the keratin invaded by fungus has been cast off by the normal turnover of skin, hair or nails. The rate of turnover of skin is about 28 days, hence the drug should be taken for at least 5 weeks. Hair can be cut to remove the infection as it grows out; fingernails take about 6 months, and toenails well over a year, to grow.

The absorption of Griseofulvin from the grastro-intestinal tract is increased in the presence of fat, such as butter, so it is better to take the drug during meals. The action of the drug is destroyed by barbiturates so these two drugs should not be given at the same time. Since Griseofulvin is not killing the fungus, it is wise to use a fungicidal local application at the same time to reduce indiscriminate shedding of infected keratin.

CHAPTER XII

INFECTIOUS DISEASES

Approximately 90,000 children of school age were recorded by the Registrar General in 1969 as suffering from a notifiable disease: in 1970, slightly over 156,000 notifications were received, the increase being mainly due to the outbreak of measles in that year. Measles, infectious hepatitis, scarlet fever, and dysentery between them account for 95% of the notifications in children in the age group 5–14 years.

Measles continues to head the list of notifiable diseases with 142,111 notifications in England and Wales in 1969, and 307,318 notifications in 1970, the rise in incidence in 1970, being due to the late summer epidemic in that year. The majority of these notifications relate to children under 5 years; in 1969, only 52,313 notifications were received for the 5–14 year age group. Whooping cough is much less prevalent in schools than formerly, with 1,659 notifications in 1969 and 7,013 in 1970. The antigen available against whooping cough is less certainly effective, but the measles vaccine could have prevented most of the large number of cases of measles. The experience of Oxford where the large majority of children are immunised is in sharp contrast with the country as a whole.

Scarlet fever is much less commonly reported than formerly with 16,093 notifications in 1969 and 13,135 in 1970 (all ages), about two-thirds of these patients being of school age. Infectious hepatitis has become the second most commonly notified disease of children of school age; 12,327 cases were notified in 1969 in this age group, of whom 7,652 were in the 5–9 year age group: in 1970, 10,870 children of school age were notified, 6,688 of these being in the 5–9 year age group.

Dysentery and food poisoning remain distressingly common, and as many as 7,505 children of school age were notified as suffering from dysentery and 1,272 from food poisoning in 1969; 3,258 cases of dysentery and 1,301 cases of food poisoning were recorded in 1970. Both diseases are certainly incompletely notified, and are spread by unsatisfactory hygiene, or food handling, or both.

There were 9 notifications of diphtheria in 1969 in children of school age, when with immunisation there need have been none: there were no notifications of the disease in children of school age in 1970, but the need for adequate immunisation has been emphasised by the outbreak in 1970 in an adult residential establishment for the mentally subnormal with 22 cases including 3 deaths; 2 other deaths were considered in retrospect to have been due to diphtheria. Tetanus was reported in 4 school children in each year in the period under review; poliomyelitis was notified in 2 children of school age in 1969: these figures are small but they are not satisfactory, when the effective immunisation procedures against diphtheria, tetanus and poliomyelitis could have prevented all of them.

Acute meningitis and acute encephalitis were reported in 455 children of school age in 1969, and 453 in 1970. Fee et al.[1] reviewing the subsequent progress of 18 children who had suffered from aseptic meningitis noted that their behaviour and school performance should be carefully watched, especially where seizures had been a feature of the original illness; 2 of these 18 children showed, on visuo-motor testing, abnormalities on follow-up investigation.

Tuberculosis

The incidence of tuberculosis of all forms in the school community has been steadily declining over many years, and in the period under review this trend has continued. The Joint Tuberculosis Committee of the British Thoracic and Tuberculosis Association in a report[2] quote an incidence of positive tuberculin tests greater than 2% at the age of 10 years in only one of the 6 districts investigated; it is probable, however, that there are many areas in which the incidence remains greater than this.

The number of new cases of respiratory tuberculosis reported in 1969–70, in the 5–14 year age group, for example, is slightly more than half the number reported in 1959–60. This downward trend has been even more marked in the 15–24 age group. Nevertheless, the incidence in this age group is still double that in children of school age and tuberculosis is still an important and preventable cause of morbidity in early working life. BCG vaccination given at the age of 10–13 years is a major weapon against the spread of the disease and gives a high degree of protection. Among teaching staff, the reduction in new cases of respiratory tuberculosis over the period 1960–70 has been satisfactory; slightly less than one-third the number of new cases were notified in the last year than in the first year of this period.

TABLE I

Respiratory tuberculosis. Notifications of new cases in England and Wales in certain age groups and among teachers

	5–14 years	15–24 years	Teachers (all ages)
1959 ..	1,246	4,415	115
1960 ..	1,165	3,613	107
1969 ..	626	1,423	34
1970 ..	588	1,403	32

Tuberculosis of the meninges and central nervous system was reported in 16 children of school age in 1969, and 18 in 1970. Tuberculosis of other organs was noted in 163 children of school age in 1969, and 158 in 1970. The rate of reduction of non-pulmonary tuberculosis has been slightly disappointing in recent years.

New entrants to Teacher Training Colleges and to the teaching profession are required to produce evidence of a satisfactory chest X-ray; many authorities also require this as a condition of service on transfer from another authority. Circular 3/69,[3] issued by the Department of Education and Science, stated that

---

[1] Develop. Med. Child Neurol. 1970, 12, 321–29.
[2] Medical Officer, 17.7.70, p. 48.
[3] Protection of Schoolchildren Against Tuberculosis.

chest X-ray at 3-yearly intervals was still advisable for teaching staff and for those whose employment brings them into regular contact with children. While younger teaching staff will have undergone recent radiological examination (and many of them have had BCG), an unknown number of older teaching staff may never have had an X-ray of the chest. In the general community, the greatest incidence of tuberculosis is in men in the 45–64 age group and routine chest radiography is most likely to be of value in their case. It is in the interests of the school staff in general to take advantage of the facilities which exist for periodic chest X-ray, particularly in the vulnerable 45–64 age group and in those younger staff who were found tuberculin positive at age 13 or who were not given BCG.

Immigrant children may come from communities and families with a higher incidence of tuberculosis, and should be tuberculin tested and offered BCG vaccination if found to be negative: positive reactors should be referred to a chest physician, and a follow-up investigation of school and home contacts carried out as considered appropriate. In his report for 1969[4], the Principal School Medical Officer of Leicester CB, notes that at the age of 13 years, 12·63% of indigenous school children were positive reactors on skin testing, while the figure for immigrant children (all ages) was 52·8%. In this report, 21 pupils aged 5–14 years were recorded as suffering from tuberculosis; 17 (80%) of these 21 pupils were immigrant children.

In 1969 over 600 pupils had their school career interrupted by respiratory tuberculosis, with the loss of valuable learning time. It is obviously important to diagnose the onset of the disease as early as possible in these children. Immediate intensive investigations of the origin of infection of all new cases arising in school are essential. The most likely source of infection is a home contact, but a hitherto undetected case of the disease in a member of the staff or even a fellow pupil may come to light, as may secondary infections. Investigation of home and school contacts is, therefore, essential.

Sporadic outbreaks of tuberculosis still occur in schools. In general, the number of pupils involved tends to be small, and there is little evidence to suggest that the infection is widely disseminated by an infected pupil or member of staff. Nevertheless, outbreaks in which the disease is more widely spread do occur from time to time. This is illustrated by the experience of a county borough school health service following the notification in 1969 of respiratory tuberculosis in a teacher. Tuberculin testing was carried out on the pupils in the school, and all positive reactors and absentees were X-rayed, with the discovery of 5 active cases. All the teaching and ancillary staff were X-rayed with negative results. The school was revisited 3 months later, when all children previously tuberculin negative were tested again: on this occasion 4 pupils had converted to positive, and one was found on X-ray examination to be a case of miliary disease. The school was revisited after a further 3 months when those children who had been negative on previous testing were again skin tested; on this occasion no child showed a positive reaction.

Certain groups of children have an increased risk of contracting tuberculosis. These include children who have been in recent contact with the disease or who have a family history of tuberculosis, and those who have large reactions or recent conversion on skin testing. Diabetic and immigrant children, and other

---

[4] Leicester C.B., Report of the School Health Service 1969.

children with persistent and prolonged ill-health, particularly with symptoms of a respiratory condition, should be carefully examined and referred to a physician for investigation.

Poliomyelitis

Immunisation against poliomyelitis using an inactivated virus vaccine began in 1956, and in 1962 live attenuated polio virus vaccine given by mouth was introduced and quickly superseded the inactivated vaccine. The live vaccine is safe and effective and has the considerable advantage of easy administration particularly in young children. Since the introduction of these vaccines, the incidence of poliomyelitis has decreased sharply; in the years immediately preceding the introduction of these vaccines, the annual number of notifications ranged between one thousand and seven thousand, and death between one hundred and seven hundred. In the period under review, there has been no outbreak of poliomyelitis, but sporadic cases still occur. The Registrar General recorded 10 cases of acute poliomyelitis in 1969, of which 2 were children of school age; there were 6 cases (all ages) of the disease in 1970. Nevertheless, despite the considerable improvement in the incidence of the disease, too many children remain unvaccinated or incompletely vaccinated. A report by Miller and his colleagues from the Public Health Laboratory Service reviewing the disease in 1965–68 in England and Wales, showed that a considerable proportion of the small number of cases of acute poliomyelitis occurs in infants and children of school age; furthermore, in the group of unvaccinated or incompletely vaccinated persons developing the disease, these were more frequently left with residual paralysis. Exposure to infection with wild virus in this country may be infrequent now, so long as the majority of pupils are vaccinated, but many children and adults will go to other countries where they are far more likely to be infected by a wild virus, and none should be denied the solid protection of vaccination.

Children on entry to school should have a course of 3 doses of oral vaccine at specified intervals if unvaccinated or not fully vaccinated; a further booster dose should be given to those children who have not been fully immunised in infancy. It is probable that most areas of England and Wales have a level of vaccination which is high enough, if maintained, to prevent a major outbreak, but there may still be pockets of unprotected individuals among whom infection would spread. The Netherlands has recently experienced just such an incident in a village where the number of objectors to vaccination was high. Neither the community nor parents can afford to neglect vaccination.

Infectious Hepatitis

This disease is a generalised infection which produces acute inflammation of the liver. It commonly has an incubation period of 30–35 days with extremes of 10 and 50 days. It is spread by person to person contact, and outbreaks, sometimes widespread, continue to occur in schools, particularly in nursery and residential schools. Young children are especially liable to contact the disease (often in an anicteric form) because of their lack of hygiene experience. The clinical picture is usually of a mild illness, and there may even be negligible symptoms without jaundice; occasionally there is a fulminating illness ending in coma and death, or a slow recovery complicated by the development of chronic hepatitis or cirrhosis. Infective jaundice, now notifiable, has become a common complaint of children of school age, being second only, among the notifiable diseases, to measles.

Most patients have a prodromal period of several days malaise and abdominal discomfort before the appearance of jaundice: nausea, anorexia and headaches are common. In most children, the illness is mild; the pre-icteric stage may last for as long as a week, and be followed by jaundice, with the usual features of dark urine, pale faeces and itching of the skin. The whole illness may last up to a month but is usually much less. There is no specific treatment. Anicteric cases are frequent particularly in younger children; these patients may have minimal or no symptoms, and the diagnosis is only confirmed on biochemical examination. Considerable investigation has been carried out on the virology of the disease; as yet no vaccine is available.

During an outbreak of infectious hepatitis in school, a strict review of all sanitary and catering arrangements, with particular attention to personal hygiene of patients and contacts (especially those handling food) is essential. Frequent medical inspections of those at risk of developing the disease may discover early or mild cases. Pupils suffering from the disease should be excluded for at least 7 days following the appearance of the jaundice, or until clinical recovery.

Human immunoglobulin is increasingly being used in the control of outbreaks, particularly in communities such as residential schools. Evidence is now accumulating that immunoglobulin is effective in controlling outbreaks of infectious hepatitis. An outbreak occurred in a residential school in the north of England in 1969 in which a pupil returned to the school after a vacation, incubating the disease. Following the development of jaundice in this child, 2 other children developed the disease, at which point, immunoglobulin was given to all children and all members of staff; no further cases were thereafter reported. Pether et al.[5] have described an outbreak in a village school, which appeared to be successfully controlled by human immunoglobulin.

Typhoid and Paratyphoid Fevers

In England and Wales, just over 100 persons (all ages) suffer from typhoid fever each year, and more than half of these infections are usually contracted abroad. In 1969, 29 children of school age contracted typhoid fever, and 23 paratyphoid fever; in 1970 there were 29 notifications of typhoid fever, and 65 of paratyphoid fever.

Educational visits to the Continent and North Africa are increasingly sponsored by Education Authorities for parties of school children, who may be at risk of contracting typhoid or paratyphoid infections and should, therefore, be fully immunised against these diseases. Principal school medical officers should, therefore, be fully informed, well in advance, of any proposed school visit abroad, so that suitable arrangements can be made to provide pupils with the appropriate immunisations. Advance warning by the organisers of such school tours, giving details of dates and destinations, is valuable, as the principal school medical officer may be in a position to advise on the suitability or otherwise of visiting a specific location.

---

[5] Medical Officer, 25.9.70: p. 165.

Carrier states, as in the population in general, may also occur in school children. Development of a carrier state in a pupil should not necessarily be considered a reason for prolonged absence from school: each case should be reviewed on its individual merits in deciding the time of readmission to school, taking into consideration the local circumstances, training in personal hygiene of the child, and banning the handling or serving of food or milk by the pupil.

Food Poisoning

Food poisoning continues to occur in schools; usually the illness is mild, but occasional outbreaks are noted in which large numbers of staff and pupils suffer more severe symptoms. The most common causative organisms are the Salmonella group and *Cl. welchii*; *Staphylococci* are less frequently incriminated.

The School Meals Service produces 5 million meals daily for school children and it is probably the largest catering service in the country. Episodes of food poisoning are very small in number when one considers the number of meals produced each year. It is of the utmost importance that the staff in charge of school kitchens constantly keep in mind the basic precepts of food hygiene.

There should be rigid adherence to the strictest standards of hygiene, both personal and of premises, and meals should be adequately cooked to ensure the death of bacteria, or effectively refrigerated to prevent bacterial growth. School kitchens should have larders or pantries to promote the rapid cooling of foodstuffs prior to these being stored in a refrigerator or refrigeration room. It is important that in any refrigeration space the temperature be effective in inhibiting bacterial growth. This was demonstrated in an outbreak of food poisoning which occurred in Northamptonshire in October 1970, in which a total of 134 pupils and staff were affected. Three schools (one secondary and two primary) were involved in the outbreak, in which each person affected had eaten a meal prepared in the kitchen of the secondary school. A total of 15 cases were admitted to hospital, 3 of which were classified as severe. The clinical features were colic, vomiting and prostration, occurring 3–4 hours after ingestion of the meal. Because of the short interval bacterial food poisoning due to enterotoxin was thought to be the most likely case; further investigation suggested the sweet course as the vehicle. A cook was found to be a nasal carrier of staphylococci.

The sweet had been prepared the day prior to its consumption and had been placed in a refrigeration room. The medical officer in charge of this investigation noted that the temperature of the room appeared to be higher than the exterior, and that uncovered heating pipes, and the heating apparatus for the hall next door, were sited along one wall. Temperature recordings over the next few days confirmed that the 'refrigeration room' was warmer than the pantry and 20°–25°C warmer than the external temperature. In this outbreak, the refrigeration room was inefficient, and must have contributed to the growth of the bacteria which caused the outbreak. Since then effective insulation has reduced the temperature in this room to acceptable limits.

High standards of personal hygiene of both kitchen staff and school children are essential in preventing food poisoning. School kitchens should have adequate toilet provision for the staff, and pupils should be encouraged to wash their hands before meals and after using the toilet. An outbreak of *S. typhimurium* in April 1970, in a boys' school is reported in which 45 people were affected.[6] In this episode, the caterer was a symptomless excreter, the meals being prepared on her premises and transported to the school, where the meals were then reheated. It was noted that there was no wash-handbasin in the kitchen toilet, and no separate hand-washing facilities in the kitchen.

Rubella Prophylaxis

Rubella is normally a mild illness with few complications. The main risk of the disease is to the foetus, if the mother is infected in the first 4 months of pregnancy. Infection of the foetus at this stage of development can cause such congenital abnormalities as cataract, deafness, cardiac lesions or mental defect, either singly or in combination. Subclinical attacks of rubella may occur without the appearance of a rash; in one report[7] 40% of patients had no rash but were shown to have rubella by isolation of the virus.

Children who develop rubella while in school should be excluded until clinical recovery, and should not, in any case, return to school before 4 days after the onset of the rash. Female members of staff, who have not had the disease, and who are in the early stages of pregnancy, should be advised not to attend school during an outbreak of rubella, until the period of infection has passed.

Many girls acquire the disease naturally in childhood, but approximately 15% of women of child-bearing age are still susceptible to rubella. Because of the high risk of congenital defects in children born to women who contract rubella in early pregnancy, an effective and safe vaccine against the disease is obviously desirable. In 1970 the use of live attenuated virus vaccine was introduced, under local health authority arrangements, for girls between their 11th and 14th birthdays, irrespective of their history of past infection. This vaccine has been shown to produce a satisfactory antibody response in 97% of persons vaccinated, and to have negligible side effects in the age group. The age at which routine vaccination is given is important, as immunity may decrease if given too early. The child-bearing age should be avoided as the possibility exists that the vaccine virus may affect the foetus. Circular CMO 9/70[8] deals with rubella prophylaxis and gives advice on the use and storage of live attenuated rubella virus for routine immunisation.

Measles Prophylaxis

Measles is a common infection of pre- and infant school age, most children having had the disease before the end of their infant schooling. Measles and its complications cause much serious illness even though the majority of children suffer only a short sharp attack. Epidemics of the disease occur every other winter, and many thousands of children develop complications; an enquiry by the Public Health Laboratory Service in 1963, assessed the incidence of serious complications to be 1 in 15 cases of the disease. The number of notifications in a year, from midsummer to midsummer, may be of the order of three quarters of a million. Although the mortality of measles in England and Wales has fallen

---

[6] Brit. Med. Journ., 17.10.70: p. 185.
[7] Brit. Med. Journ., 2.5.70.
[8] DHSS: CMO 9/70: issued 29.7.70.

progressively it has remained at a level of 100 per year. In developing countries, measles is still one of the great killing diseases of childhood in the absence of vaccination. Immunity resulting from an attack of measles is probably life-long in most cases.

In 1968, a national mass-vaccination campaign against measles was introduced, but this had subsequently to be slowed down, as one of the 2 vaccines being used was withdrawn following the reports of a higher incidence of adverse reactions. Nevertheless, substantial numbers of children were vaccinated, and the number of children developing measles in 1969, a year in which a high incidence would have been expected, as well below the anticipated level. This decline, however, was followed by a sharp rise in the notifications of measles in the summer months of 1970 and in that year, notifications were at about half the level of an epidemic year. This summer epidemic, together with the availability of new supplies of satisfactory vaccine, has prompted an increased demand for measles vaccination, but acceptance is still well below the level required for control. Vaccination against measles is given by one injection (preferably in the second year). Some children develop a mild febrile reaction, and occasionally a rash 7–10 days after vaccination, but severe reactions are very rare.

Memorandum on the Control of Infectious Diseases in Schools

The Department of Education and Science has recently issued the above memorandum, which deals with communicable diseases occurring in school children. It is an advisory document and is for the information of medical officers only; it is not intended to act as a guide for teaching staff. Principal school medical officers are recommended to provide a simplified extract for use by their local education authorities.

The memorandum reviews the procedures for obtaining information about communicable disease in school and recommends 'that Principal School Medical Officers make clear and definite arrangements whereby they may be informed of suspected or confirmed cases of communicable disease'. The action to be taken in cases of communicable disease in school children is reviewed in respect of general measures, exclusion of individual pupils, liaison with other medical officers, school closure, exclusion of staff, teachers with pulmonary tuberculosis and school meals staff.

Brief notes and suggestions for action on specific communicable diseases are included in the memorandum and Table I provides information on the incubation, and exclusion periods of the commoner communicable diseases. Similar brief notes and suggestions are provided for contagious skin conditions, while Table II lists exclusion periods for some commoner skin infections.

CHAPTER XIII

THE SCHOOL DENTAL SERVICE

In a report on the Dental Health of the Adult Population,[1] published in 1968, the point was made that the present poor condition of the teeth of the older members of the community was the consequence of inadequate dental care when they were children. The report referred in particular to deficiencies in the school dental services, which were in fact the main source of treatment for children in the years preceding and during the Second World War, and in support of this argument quoted some of the directives issued at that time by the Ministry of Education, for the guidance of dental officers working in the local authority dental services. However stark and uncompromising this advice appears now, the conditions and circumstances prevailing at the time it was issued should not be lost sight of. Faced with the task of providing treatment for an excessively large number of children, the meagre resources of the school dental services in many localities resulted in the extraction rather than the conservation of decayed teeth and despite the reduction of caries attributable to the wartime shortage of sugar, the results of this unavoidable policy were very evident to the dentists who conducted the examinations for the 1968 epidemiological survey.

The resources available for the dental treatment of children have substantially improved in recent years. In 1969 the number of dental officers, dental auxiliaries and hygienists working in the local authority services was higher than it has ever been, and this enabled a record number of sessions to be devoted to the dental treatment of children. In addition to the work of the school dental officers, over $5\frac{1}{2}$ million courses of dental treatment were provided for children up to and including those aged fifteen, by general dental surgeons working in the National Health Service in contract with executive councils. The amount of dental treatment for children has been steadily increasing over the past seventeen years, with a general improvement in the ratio of teeth filled to those extracted, and the provision of a wider range of dental treatment for children than was possible some years ago.

Despite this very real improvement, there is no room for complacency. The increase in the school population which will take place over the next few years can only accentuate present difficulties, and the report on the dental condition of some 15,000 fifteen-year-old children who were examined in 1965, which is described in Appendix A, is a sharp reminder that although almost all the children had received some dental treatment, they still had a considerable number of teeth which required attention.

The average number of teeth requiring fillings at age fifteen was found to be 4, and this is indeed higher than that (1·8) found to be required by those adults who are still in possession of some of their natural teeth, and who were ex-

---

[1] Government Social Survey, 'Adult Dental Health in England and Wales in 1968.'

amined in the course of the Adult Dental Health survey. The explanation for this apparent anomaly, apart from the time lapse between the two surveys, is that the adults had lost 10 teeth, whilst the fifteen-year-olds had on average only 1·8 teeth missing.

Dental Health Education

In a recent publication on dental health education[2] (World Health Organization Report No. 449), drawn up by an expert committee of the World Health Organization, some older concepts of health education are examined. In discussing dental health education in schools, the report states: 'Those programmes have been essentially of the "information-giving" type and their informational content has almost always been the same. Furthermore, programmes of teacher education focused on improving the status of dental health education have employed this same approach. In spite of the overwhelming evidence that providing teachers and children with information about dental health is not an effective method of obtaining behavioural change, this approach has continued to predominate.' In this connection a working party of the Health Education Council[3] drew attention to the inadequacy of evaluation of the results of dental health education campaigns.

Almost all local authorities carry out some form of dental health education, ranging from short-term intensive campaigns to systematic talks to children at school. Some issue free toothbrushes, paste and beakers to children attending school for the first time, and most of them display posters designed to attract attention to the benefits accruing from regular toothbrushing and the practice of sound dietary principles.

Whatever the merits of any particular form of dental health education directed to changing the dietary and oral hygiene habits of the population, there can be no misgivings about the measures directed to stressing the fundamental importance of regular attendances for dental inspection and treatment. In this respect the dental officers of the local authority services are in a unique position with their opportunity for screening children at child-welfare centres, when they first attend school, and during their school life. Such examinations to establish the child's need for treatment enable parents to be made aware of their children's dental needs and as long as efforts are made to ensure that children do in fact obtain treatment—the source of the treatment is immaterial—in the long term the school dentist must always be the keystone of this vital form of education in dental health. Following initiation of dental treatment, a patient's willingness to become a regular attender would seem to depend on the ability of the individual dentist to earn the confidence of his patient and in the case of children, of the child's parents. It is when this rapport has been established that advice on diet and oral hygiene would appear to have the best chance of success.

Accommodation and Equipment

The standard of dental equipment and accommodation in the local authority services is steadily improving and there are many fine clinics in operation today.

---

[2] Dental Health Education, 'Report of a WHO Expert Committee,' No 449, 1970.
[3] Dental Health Education, 'A report presented by a working group' R. O. Walker, H. C. Davis, R. Emslie, G. H. Leatherman and G. Sheon, April 1969.

To assist authorities in the provision of new dental departments and the replacement of out of date establishments, the Department of Health and Social Security published in November 1970 a design guide[4] on health centres, which contains useful information about dental accommodation. Taking account of the recent technological developments and the streamlining of many dental procedures, the diagrams in the guide suggest a flexible approach to surgery design which will cater for several possible individual preferences.

The Mentally-handicapped Child

Under the Education (Handicapped Pupils) Act 1970 responsibility for the education of mentally handicapped children, hitherto borne by the health authorities, was transferred to the education service, and local education authority responsibilities for dental inspection and treatment now apply to them as well as to other school children. A preliminary report by a Guy's Hospital research team, which has been undertaking treatment of handicapped children in the London Boroughs of Southwark, Lewisham and Greenwich, concludes that most of them are able to receive conservative treatment without resort having to be made to general anaesthesia.

Thamesmead. As part of Guy's Hospital General Practice Research, a dental unit integrating the services provided by the local authority and the executive council, has been in operation at Thamesmead since 1969. Experience gained in this pilot study, which is already treating some school children in the London Boroughs of Bexley and Greenwich, will be of value if the projected reorganisation of the National Health Service comes about.

Fluoridation

Although some 3,000,000 people in England and Wales are now drinking water to which fluoride has been added, the slow progress being made in the general adoption of fluoridation has led many local authorities to enquire into the efficacy of other methods of obtaining the dental benefits provided by the addition of fluoride to water supplies. Fluoridation provides on a community basis both systemic and topical effects throughout the life of the individual. These are complementary, and both are necessary if the optimum benefit is to be obtained.

Many of the alternatives provide either topical or systemic effect, but not both, and rely on individual initiative, a weakness which makes them a poor substitute for community measures; and consideration must be given to their defects before methods which are prodigal of professional time and resources and which may not be entirely suited to the local circumstances, are adopted. To be effective the systemic administration of fluoride requires daily ingestion of small quantities during the years of tooth calcification—from birth to about twelve years of age. When individual families are prepared to undertake the continuous unbroken routine which this demands, the results are known to be excellent but there will be few such families. Reports on the issue of free fluoride tablets as a community health measure in Tasmania and New Jersey indicate that in the end very few families availed themselves of the offer.

The results obtained by topical methods of application, many of which are particularly demanding of professional time, and which only confer transient

---

[4] DHSS, Health Centres—A Design Guide, H.M.S.O.

benefit, vary widely, and some reports may be misleading as they refer to incremental reductions of caries, that is, the reduction in the number of new carious lesions appearing during the limited period of investigation. These figures should not be confused with those referring to reductions in the cumulative amount of dental caries experienced at stated ages which are available in reports of studies of water fluoridation.

APPENDIX A

DENTAL STATUS OF THE 15-YEAR-OLD SCHOOL CHILD IN ENGLAND AND WALES

The Sample

A survey of the dental health of 15-year-old school children in England and Wales was undertaken by school dental officers during the spring term 1965. To keep the burden on the service and the cost of mounting the exercise to a minimum it was necessary to adopt a two-stage sampling method. Efforts were made, nevertheless, to ensure a representative sample and the accurate and consistent recording of the condition of the teeth and gums and of other clinical and general information. Nearly 15,500 pupil-examinations were conducted in 30 local education authorities.

The 30 authorities invited to take part in the survey were chosen to form a representative sample of authorities in terms of geographical spread and urban/rural characteristics. West Hartlepool was included because of the presence of natural fluoride in the water there.

The survey was conducted by the school dental officers in each authority, who examined a sample of children in every maintained secondary and all-age school. In Cardiff, one of the Welsh authorities selected, the survey was mistakenly restricted to secondary modern schools.

Individual pupils were selected according to date of birth. Those born on 5, 15 or 25 of each month from August 1949 to July 1950, inclusive, were chosen.

The sample was incomplete so far as August-born children were concerned in as much as some of these children whose fifteenth birthdays fell between 1 August and 1 September 1964, inclusive (i.e. had attained statutory leaving age at the end of the summer term 1964), would either not have returned to school in September 1964 or, having returned, might have left before the survey took place.

The theoretical sampling proportion within each authority resulting from this method would be approximately 9·5%, taking into account the loss of some August-born children. In fact, the overall sample achieved in this survey was 8·5%. Twenty-seven of the 30 authorities produced samples ranging from 11.3% to 7·8%. These results are within the probable variations from the theoretical mean of 9·5% and match very well the actual results achieved in other surveys using this sampling method. There is every reason to suppose that these samples were correctly drawn and well-covered in the clinical examinations. The incomplete Cardiff sample has already been mentioned. From the remaining two authorities samples of 5·9% and 5·4% emerged. In these cases it is highly probable that children were lost from the sample, through lack of co-operation on the part of children or parents, or because of inadequate liaison between the school dental service and the schools.

Table I gives the number of children examined in each participating authority.

98

TABLE I

15-YEAR-OLD DENTAL SURVEY, 1965—PUPILS EXAMINED

	Modern schools		Grammar schools		All other secondary schools		All schools		
	Boys	Girls	Boys	Girls	Boys	Girls	Boys	Girls	Boys & Girls
Northern Region									
Cheshire	331	279	164	183	(1)	2	495	464	959
Lancashire	933	818	247	235	58	30	1,238	1,083	2,321
Northumberland	223	199	48	55	5	7	276	261	537
Yorkshire:									
North Riding	165	159	42	39	20	11	227	209	436
Bradford	121	105	56	47	19	10	196	162	358
Dewsbury	26	35	7	6	4	5	37	46	83
Manchester	232	211	55	42	65	64	352	317	669
Sheffield	167	157	60	35	49	35	276	227	503
Southport	29	14	15	14	3	(1)	47	28	75
Wallasey	42	37	17	15	—	—	59	52	111
York	54	49	18	9	(1)	(1)	72	58	130
Total	2,323	2,063	729	680	223	164	3,275	2,907	6,182
Midland Region									
Derbyshire	327	312	97	90	28	16	452	418	870
Nottinghamshire	248	222	53	45	54	48	355	315	670
Staffordshire	340	301	79	91	33	38	452	430	882
Birmingham	244	283	51	81	49	48	344	412	756
Lincoln	13	24	12	15	(1)	(1)	25	39	64
Nottingham	59	53	26	35	102	83	187	171	358
Smethwick	21	21	13	11	7	(1)	41	32	73
Wolverhampton	68	55	15	20	25	28	108	103	211
Total	1,320	1,271	346	388	298	261	1,964	1,920	3,884
Southern Region									
Devon	224	167	41	63	26	17	291	247	538
Hertfordshire	300	285	94	96	21	18	415	399	814
Somerset	225	200	63	62	6	2	294	264	558
Surrey	343	310	111	114	146	215	600	639	1,239
Bristol	69	74	44	36	125	176	238	286	524
Ipswich	61	63	7	7	(1)	(1)	68	70	138
Norwich	50	60	22	16	(1)	(1)	72	76	148
Total	1,272	1,159	382	394	324	428	1,978	1,981	3,959
Wales									
Caernarvonshire	27	33	19	26	15	8	61	67	128
Glamorgan	309	254	136	153	39	30	484	437	921
Cardiff	117	113	(2)	(2)	(2)	(1)	117	113	230
Total	453	400	155	179	54	38	662	617	1,279
Totals: England	4,915	4,493	1,457	1,462	845	853	7,217	6,808	14,025
England and Wales (except West Hartlepool)	5,368	4,893	1,612	1,641	899	891	7,879	7,425	15,304
West Hartlepool	39	24	7	11	11	8	57	43	100
England and Wales (including West Hartlepool)	5,407	4,917	1,619	1,652	910	899	7,936	7,468	15,404

(1) No 'Other' secondary schools existed.
(2) School population not sampled.

The samples of pupils, with the exception of Cardiff and the two under-sampled authorities, were quasi-random samples and representative of the individual authorities' 15-year-old pupils. But in calculating results for regions and for England and Wales as a whole it was necessary to introduce a weighting system into the grossing-up of the total sample. This was because the authorities chosen in a particular region did not necessarily have the same balance of sexes and types of school as in the region as a whole, and it was to be expected that there would be a variation in the clinical data with both sex of child and type of school. Grossing-up factors were therefore calculated for each sex, type of

99

school and region. Because of the natural fluoride in the West Hartlepool water supply, this authority was excluded from regional and national calculations.

This method of arriving at regional and national figures relies on the assumption that the 15-year-old children in the chosen authorities in a region were, sex for sex and school type for school type, representative of the region as a whole. Quite apart from the errors arising from quasi-random sampling within the individual authorities' populations, the regional and national data produced are therefore as reliable as that assumption is valid.

The Dental Examination

The large number of dental officers involved in the survey made calibration of the charting of individual examining dentists unrealistic, but clear and simple guidance was given to ensure that the examinations were conducted in good light with the aid of mirror and expendable probes. Probes were discarded after each twenty examinations, a uniform method of charting was followed and entries were made on a standard chart. The result represents the opinion of dentists, specially experienced in the treatment of children, as to how much treatment had been given to each child and how much more would be required in practice to render him dentally fit.

TABLE II

THE SOURCE OF TREATMENT

Percentage of children in the survey who received previous treatment from	School dental service	General dental service	Other sources of treatment	Received no previous treatment
Girls				
Secondary modern schools ..	30·8	65·4	1·8	1·7
Grammar schools	11·6	86·6	1·4	0·3
Other schools	21·5	75·4	1·9	1·1
Total	25·3	71.4	1·8	1·3
Boys				
Secondary modern schools ..	32·9	61·6	2·8	2·5
Grammar schools	15·5	82·3	1·5	0·8
Other schools	28·8	67·0	2·1	2·0
Total	28·9	66·5	2·3	2·1

Most children obtain their dental treatment from the school dental service or the general dental service, but a few are treated in hospitals or by dental officers of the Armed Forces overseas or by dental surgeons practising outside the health service. Some 15-year-olds will have had treatment from more than one source, but in this survey the examining dentists only enquired where their most recent course of treatment had been carried out. The figures in Table II show that only a very small proportion of children had not previously been treated (this was especially true for grammar school pupils) and that the source of treatment for children appears to vary with the type of school they attend. There are also marginal differences which can be attributed to their sex.

The Condition of the Teeth

Dental officers conducting the examination were required to account for all the teeth present in the mouth, which were classified as to the number of teeth

requiring filling	D1
requiring extraction	D2
missing	M
which had been satisfactorily filled	F

It should be noted that some teeth in category D1 had been previously filled but required further attention.

TABLE III

DMF VALUES FOR 15-YEAR-OLDS IN ALL REGIONS

	D1	D2	M	F	DMF
Boys	4·2	0·4	1·7	3·5	9·8
Girls	3·8	0·4	1·9	4·4	10·5
Boys and Girls ..	4·0	0·4	1·8	4·0	10·1

The figures demonstrate that there is a slight difference in total DMF between the sexes and that boys had more teeth requiring filling and had a smaller number of teeth satisfactorily filled than girls.

A further breakdown of these figures into the type of school which the pupils attended in each region is given in Table IV.

TABLE IV

	Grammar schools					Secondary modern schools				
	D1	D2	M	F	DMF	D1	D2	M	F	DMF
Region										
Northern ..	3·1	0·2	1·8	5·0	10·2	3·9	0·5	2·0	3·2	9·6
Midlands ..	3·6	0·3	1·7	4·9	10·5	4·7	0·5	1·8	2·7	9·8
Southern ..	3·0	0·1	1·2	6·2	10·4	3·4	0·3	1·4	5·2	10·2
Wales	6·2	0·4	2·2	3·6	12·4	7·0	0·8	2·5	2·1	12·4
England and Wales ..	3·5	0·2	1·7	5·1	10·6	4·3	0·5	1·8	3·5	10·0

It is apparent that whilst there are sizeable differences in the total DMF rates between regions, within any one region the differences attributable to the type of school attended are not large. There is however evidence that in every region grammar school pupils have more satisfactorily-filled teeth, have fewer teeth requiring filling and have fewer missing teeth than have secondary modern school pupils.

Oral Hygiene and Gingivitis

Examining officers were asked to classify the oral hygiene of the children examined as good, fair or poor, and to say whether gingivitis was absent, mild or severe.

TABLE V

ORAL HYGIENE (PERCENTAGE OF CHILDREN EXAMINED)

	Grammar schools			Secondary modern schools		
	Good	Fair	Poor	Good	Fair	Poor
Region						
Northern ..	65	30	5	44	40	16
Midlands ..	63	32	5	48	38	14
Southern ..	65	30	5	52	38	11
Wales	49	40	11	42	40	18
Average for England and Wales ..	64	31	5	48	39	14

Within every region more grammar school pupils had good oral hygiene and fewer had poor oral hygiene than those in secondary modern schools. The standard of oral hygiene in Wales appeared to be lower than that in England.

TABLE VI

GINGIVITIS (PERCENTAGE OF CHILDREN EXAMINED)

	Grammar schools			Secondary modern schools		
	Absent	Mild	Severe	Absent	Mild	Severe
Region						
Northern ..	74·4	24·6	1·0	66·2	31·4	2·4
Midlands ..	78·4	20·8	0·8	68·8	29·5	1·7
Southern ..	75·4	24·2	0·4	68·4	29·6	2·0
Wales	68·6	29·9	1·5	62·6	34·8	2·6

TABLE VII

RELATIONSHIP BETWEEN ORAL HYGIENE AND GINGIVITIS

	Gingivitis		
Oral hygiene	Absent	Mild	Severe
Good	91·2	8·7	0·1
Fair	53·0	46·1	0·9
Poor	21·0	67·4	11·6

As might have been expected mild to severe gingivitis occurred most frequently among those whose standard of oral hygiene was rated 'Poor' (Table VII).

TABLE VIII

DENTAL CONDITION IN WEST HARTLEPOOL COMPARED WITH AVERAGE FOR ENGLAND AND WALES

	D1	D2	M	F	DMF
England and Wales	4·0	0·4	1·8	4·0	10·1
West Hartlepool	2·8	0·2	0·8	2·0	5·7

TABLE IX

	DMF	DMF 1–5	DMF 6–10	DMF 11–15	DMF 16–20	DMF Over 20
Region						
Northern ..	1	15	45	28	9	1
Midlands ..	1	13	44	30	9	1
Southern ..	0	11	44	30	10	1
Wales	0	4	31	37	21	4
West Hartlepool	6	42	43	8	1	0

The average DMF value for 15-year-old children in West Hartlepool, where there is a natural fluoride content of 1–2 ppm in the water, was slightly over half that recorded for the rest of the country.

The ratio of general dental service dentists to the population in West Hartlepool is 1:8740 and the ratio of school dental officers to schoolchildren is 1:7200, compared respectively with 1:4500 and 1:5400 in the rest of England and Wales.

It will be seen from Table VIII that, although only half the number of teeth were filled and extracted in West Hartlepool compared with the rest of the country, the amount of treatment required was still a good deal less. When the proportion of children with similar DMF scores are compared (Table IX), the superiority of the dental condition of West Hartlepool children is convincingly demonstrated.

Conclusions

This survey of a large number of 15-year-old children was carried out in 1965. Since then, more sophisticated examination procedures for dental epidemiological enquiries have been evolved. It is probable that in any future survey of this kind representative sampling could be achieved by the examination of a much smaller number of children.

APPENDIX B

STATISTICS OF THE SCHOOL HEALTH SERVICE

TABLE I

STAFF OF THE SCHOOL HEALTH SERVICE

	Medical Officers												Nurses and Health Visitors					
	Solely school health service		Part-time school health service/rest of time local health service		Part-time school health service/rest of time as general practitioner		Part-time school health service of time on other medical work		Ophthalmic specialists		Other consultants and specialists		With health visitors' certificate		Without health visitors' certificate		Nurses' assistants	
	f.t.	p.t.	f.t.	p.t.	f.t.	p.t.	f.t.	p.t.	f.t.	p.t.	f.t.	p.t.	f.t.	p.t.	f.t.	p.t.	f.t.	p.t.
Number:																		
1969 England	123	60	939	696	—	705	21	452	3	249	—	196	3,425	2,755	1,076	1,379	271	156
Wales	1	2	120	32	—	21	18	14	—	6	—	5	426	73	130	54	13	11
Total	124	62	1,059	728	—	726	39	466	3	255	—	201	3,851	2,828	1,206	1,433	284	167
Number:																		
1970 England	113	71	942	792	—	695	7	449	3	253	—	193	4,074	2,296	1,208	1,207	294	323
Wales	3	2	114	40	—	23	11	18	—	8	—	3	438	66	135	74	13	12
Total	116	73	1,056	832	—	718	18	467	3	261	—	196	4,512	2,362	1,343	1,281	307	335
Whole-time equivalent:																		
1969 England	137·2		599·5		89·5		81·9		55·2		18·0		1,888·0		1,272·7		219·4	
Wales	1·2		60·0		2·5		9·1		0·5		0·3		124·0		49·9		12·0	
Total	138·4		659·5		92·0		91·0		55·7		18·3		2,012·0		1,322·6		231·4	
Whole-time equivalent:																		
1970 England	134·5		687·2		85·1		80·6		55·7		17·2		1,735·6		1,349·2		342·6	
Wales	3·1		57·2		2·9		7·1		7·0		0·1		166·4		61·7		12·5	
Total	137·6		744·4		88·0		87·7		62·7		17·3		1,902·0		1,410·9		355·1	

TABLE I—*continued*

STAFF OF THE SCHOOL HEALTH SERVICE

	Speech Therapists															
	Senior speech therapists		Speech therapists		Assistant speech therapists		Audio-metricians		Chiropodists		Orthoptists		Physio-therapists		Others (excluding clerical staff)	
	f.t.	p.t.	f.t.	p.t.	f.t.	p.t.	f.t.	p.t.	f.t.	p.t.	f.t.	p.t.	f.t.	p.t.	f.t.	p.t.
Number: 1969 England	67	17	253	314	—	2	82	62	47	167	9	51	120	172	103	71
Wales ..	4	3	15	10	1	—	1	5	—	—	—	3	1	2	1	—
Total ..	71	20	268	324	1	2	83	67	47	161	9	54	121	174	104	71
Number: 1970 England	65	25	270	345	1	4	79	66	58	168	10	53	116	165	100	90
Wales ..	5	2	13	12	1	—	3	5	—	2	—	3	1	2	2	—
Total ..	70	27	283	357	2	4	82	71	58	170	10	56	117	167	102	90
Whole-time equivalent: 1969 England	73·1		372·2		0·9	1·0	95·7	3·1	25·9		24·8	1·1	169·2	1·5	112·5	0·7
Wales ..	5·3		18·6						—							
Total ..	78·4		390·8		1·9		98·8		25·9		25·9		170·7		113·2	
Whole-time equivalent 1970 England	78·8		396·8		4·8	1·0	101·9	4·4	31·4	0·3	25·9	1·2	166·7	1·5	123·4	0·7
Wales ..	5·8		17·1													
Total ..	84·6		413·9		5·8		106·3		31·7		27·1		168·2		124·1	

TABLE II

STAFF OF THE SCHOOL HEALTH SERVICE—CHILD GUIDANCE AND SCHOOL PSYCHOLOGICAL SERVICE

	Psychiatrists				Educational Psychologists		Psychiatric Social Workers		Social Workers				Psycho-therapists		Remedial Teachers		Others (excluding Clerical Staff)	
	Employed by the local education authority		Employed under arrangements with hospital authority		Employed in Child Guidance Clinics	Employed in the School Psychological Service			Qualified		Unqualified							
	f.t.	p.t.	f.t.	p.t.			f.t.	p.t.	f.t.	p.t.	f.t.	p.t.	f.t.	p.t.	f.t.	p.t.	f.t.	p.t.
Number: 1969 England	8	87	14	229		498	159	119	81	86	28	28	21	79	285	539	26	52
Wales	1	3	4	15		34	5	4	10	5	5	5	—	—	35	19	—	1
Total	9	90	18	244		532	164	123	91	91	33	33	21	79	320	558	26	53
Number 1970 England	13	89	15	230		520	172	100	107	87	19	28	26	54	329	561	39	27
Wales	1	3	8	17		34	7	2	12	1	7	3	—	—	112	84	27	1
Total	14	92	23	247		554	179	102	119	88	26	31	26	54	441	645	66	28
Whole-time equivalent 1969 England	32·8	1·3	100·8	7·3	179·9 4·8	259·5 19·5	214·4	5·3	116·9	11·7	39·5	4·2	53·8	—	425·9	44·5	40·3	0·5
Total	34·6		108·1		184·7	279·0	219·7		128·6		43·7		53·8		470·4		40·8	
Whole-time equivalent 1970 England	41·0	1·8	93·1	8·0	185·4 5·0	288·2 21·3	197·0	4·2	150·7	10·0	33·3	3·6	57·6	—	496·3	154·2	49·8	27·5
Total	42·8		101·1		190·4	309·5	201·2		160·7		36·9		57·6		650·5		77·3	

106

TABLE III

MEDICAL INSPECTIONS

	Number of pupils on registers of maintained and assisted primary and secondary schools (including nursery and special schools) in January		Number of pupils inspected during the year			
			At periodic inspections		At special and re-inspections	
	1970	1971	1969	1970	1969	1970
England	7,592,906	7,788,840	1,702,121	1,687,449	1,154,841	1,121,140
Wales	487,825	496,083	94,390	98,880	60,162	58,175
	8,080,731	8,284,923	1,796,511	1,786,329	1,215,003	1,179,315

TABLE IV

RECORDED INCIDENCE OF CERTAIN DEFECTS AND DISEASES IN 1970 REQUIRING TREATMENT AND/OR OBSERVATION

Number of periodic inspections in 1970
1,786,329
Number of special inspections in 1970
477,809

Defect	Number of defects											
	Periodic Inspections						Special Inspection		Total		Total England and Wales
	Entrants		Intermediate		Leavers						
	England	Wales	England	Wales	England	Wales	England	Wales	England	Wales	
Skin	25,658	1,325	21,252	714	15,784	712	43,237	2,801	105,931	5,552	111,483
Eyes—vision	70,510	4,546	83,404	3,441	56,879	3,225	59,554	2,682	270,347	13,894	284,241
squint	21,092	1,126	9,949	539	3,316	205	6,407	461	40,764	2,331	43,095
other	4,088	251	4,113	216	2,324	136	4,684	113	15,209	716	15,925
Ear—hearing	36,521	1,659	18,733	797	5,309	372	24,586	2,153	85,149	4,981	90,130
otitis media	17,168	884	7,130	286	2,527	154	3,393	312	30,218	1,636	31,854
other	6,642	544	3,678	311	1,803	89	5,927	360	18,050	1,304	19,354
Nose and throat	53,845	4,852	26,367	1,484	8,770	813	15,016	1,418	103,998	8,567	112,565
Speech	27,460	1,311	8,946	478	1,493	95	8,480	611	46,379	2,495	48,874
Lymphatic glands	15,973	1,689	5,029	448	1,299	122	2,880	227	25,181	2,486	27,667
Heart	13,323	1,382	7,310	428	3,338	412	3,797	544	27,768	2,766	30,534
Lungs	22,963	1,296	13,561	663	5,113	323	7,564	735	49,201	3,017	52,218
Development—hernia	5,263	269	2,038	106	506	67	810	75	8,617	517	9,134
other	21,486	1,320	14,037	615	4,383	214	7,873	580	47,779	2,729	50,508
Orthopaedic—posture	4,460	390	5,578	201	3,623	239	1,837	163	15,498	993	16,491
feet	26,100	2,308	15,898	719	7,786	490	8,338	456	58,122	3,973	62,095
other	14,315	1,178	9,344	586	5,656	351	7,363	574	36,668	2,689	39,357
Nervous system—epilepsy	3,089	232	2,767	180	1,242	115	1,739	238	8,837	765	9,602
other	7,293	356	5,090	250	1,756	100	4,360	248	18,499	954	19,453
Psychological—development	14,090	543	14,711	659	3,778	228	11,979	737	44,558	2,167	46,725
stability	26,164	574	18,289	417	4,612	190	13,492	381	62,557	1,562	64,119
Abdomen	6,694	541	5,341	320	2,276	142	2,268	288	16,579	1,291	17,870
Other	20,777	598	21,131	370	8,807	372	43,395	1,006	94,110	2,346	96,456

TABLE V

| | Number of defects treated, or under treatment during the year | | | | | |
| | 1969 | | | 1970 | | |
	England	Wales	Total	England	Wales	Total
DISEASES OF THE SKIN:						
Ringworm—scalp	429	3	432	893	35	928
Ringworm—body	722	47	769	594	15	609
Scabies	17,282	1,260	18,542	17,711	1,146	18,857
Impetigo	9,468	239	9,707	8,401	167	8,568
Other skin diseases ..	147,101	3,630	150,731	132,969	2,902	135,871
EYE DISEASES: DEFECTIVE VISION AND SQUINT:						
External and others (excluding errors of refraction and squint)	28,974	628	29,602	25,200	610	25,810
Errors of refraction and squint	378,935	25,370	404,305	381,935	27,118	409,053
Number of pupils for whom spectacles were prescribed	191,310	11,058	202,368	135,230	11,156	146,386
DEFECTS OF EAR:						
Total number of pupils still on registers of school at 31 December known to have been provided with hearing aids:—						
a. during the calendar year	1,856	139	1,995	2,221	174	2,395
b. in previous years ..	11,657	614	12,271	12,278	623	12,901
CONVALESCENT TREATMENT:						
Number of pupils who received convalescent treatment under school health service arrangements ..	6,295	396	6,691	5,590	2	5,592
MINOR AILMENTS:						
Number of pupils with minor ailments	308,643	4,407	313,050	284,152	2,761	286,913

TABLE VI

NUMBER OF CHILDREN KNOWN TO HAVE RECEIVED TREATMENT
UNDER CHILD GUIDANCE ARRANGEMENTS DURING THE YEAR

	Number of clinics		Number of pupils treated	
	1969	1970	1969	1970
England ..	370	382	62,465	66,124
Wales ..	24	24	3,189	3,197
Total ..	394	406	65,654	69,321

TABLE VII

NUMBER OF CHILDREN KNOWN TO HAVE RECEIVED TREATMENT
UNDER SPEECH THERAPY ARRANGEMENTS DURING THE YEAR

	Number of clinics		Number of pupils treated	
	1969	1970	1969	1970
England ..	1,411	1,494	77,132	83,192
Wales ..	121	111	5,175	4,972
Total ..	1,532	1,605	82,307	88,164

TABLE VIII

Uncleanliness and verminous conditions found during the year

| | Total number of examinations of pupils in schools by school nurses or other authorised persons | | Total number of individual pupils found to be infested | | Number of individual pupils in respect of whom were issued | | | |
| | | | | | Cleansing Notices under Section 54 (2) of the Education Act 1944 | | Cleansing Orders under Section 54 (3) of the Education Act 1944 | |
	1969	1970	1969	1970	1969	1970	1969	1970
England ..	10,017,775	10,589,839	192,896	222,833	29,852	38,435	6,473	7,250
Wales ..	700,643	733,272	10,861	14,980	2,371	2,705	51	30
Total	10,718,418	11,323,111	203,757	237,813	32,223	41,140	6,524	7,280

TABLE IX

Causes of death	Under 5 years of age M	Under 5 years of age F	5–14 years of age M	5–14 years of age F	Total M	Total F	Total male and female
1. Enteritis and other diarrhoeal diseases ..	242	161	7	1	249	162	411
2. Tuberculosis of respiratory system ..	2	1	1	1	3	2	5
3. Other tuberculosis, including late effects ..	5	7	7	2	12	9	21
4. Diphtheria ..	—	—	—	—	—	—	—
5. Whooping cough	8	6	—	1	8	7	15
6. Meningococcal infection ..	55	40	5	8	60	48	108
7. Acute polio-myelitis ..	—	—	—	—	—	—	—
8. Measles	12	15	4	9	16	24	40
9. Syphilis and its sequelae ..	—	—	—	—	—	—	—
10. All other infective and parasitic diseases ..	104	87	1	8	105	95	200
Malignant neo-plasm of:							
11. Stomach ..	—	—	—	—	—	—	—
12. Trachea, bronchus and lung ..	—	—	—	—	—	—	—
13. Breast	—	—	—	—	—	—	—
14. Cervix uteri and other uterus ..	—	—	—	—	—	1	1
15. Leukaemia, aleukaemia ..	71	53	114	96	185	149	334
16. Other malignant neoplasms ..	102	75	32	8	134	83	217
17. Diabetes mellitus	6	4	5	6	11	10	21
18. Hypertensive disease ..	—	—	1	—	1	—	1
19. Ischaemic heart disease ..	2	4	—	—	2	4	6
20. Other forms of heart disease..	45	40	12	17	57	57	114
21. Cerebrovascular disease ..	21	17	11	16	32	33	65
22. Other circulatory diseases ..	6	8	10	7	16	15	31
23. Influenza ..	17	14	8	7	25	21	46
24. Pneumonia ..	1,064	783	71	65	1,135	848	1,983
25. Bronchitis, all forms ..	481	354	23	18	504	372	876
26. Other diseases of respiratory system ..	149	101	25	30	174	131	305
27. Peptic ulcer ..	3	4	—	1	3	5	8
28. Other diseases of digestive system ..	225	151	30	27	255	178	433
29. Nephritis and nephrosis ..	15	3	7	7	22	10	32

TABLE IX—*continued*

30. Hyperplasia of prostate ..	—	—	—	—	—	—	—
31. Complications of pregnancy, child-birth and the puerperium ..	—	—	—	—	—	—	—
32. Congenital anomalies ..	1,754	1,534	122	116	1,876	1,650	3,526
33. Other defined and ill-defined diseases ..	4,497	3,095	314	250	4,811	3,345	8,156
34. Motor vehicle accidents ..	151	77	356	149	507	226	733
35. All other accidents	487	328	290	73	777	401	1,178
36. Suicide and self-inflicted injuries	—	—	—	2	—	2	2
37. All other external causes ..	60	47	9	13	69	60	129
All causes ..	9,584	7,009	1,465	939	11,049	7,948	18,997

TABLE X

NET EXPENDITURE OF LOCAL EDUCATION AUTHORITIES ON THE SCHOOL HEALTH SERVICE FOR THE FINANCIAL YEAR 1969–1970

	Net expenditure to be met from grants and rates (excluding loan charges and capital expenditure from revenue) (£000)
England	23,129
Wales	1,476
Total	24,605

TABLE XI

NUMBERS OF CORRECTED NOTIFICATIONS OF INFECTIOUS DISEASES AMONG CHILDREN UNDER 15 DURING THE YEAR ENDED 31 DECEMBER 1970

| | Scarlet Fever | | Whooping Cough | | Acute Poliomyelitis | | | | Measles | | Diphtheria | | Dysentery | |
| | | | | | Paralytic | | Non-paralytic | | | | | | | |
	M	F	M	F	M	F	M	F	M	F	M	F	M	F
Under 5 years	1,998	1,802	4,387	4,819	1	—	—	—	91,353	87,422	—	—	1,938	1,628
5–14 years	3,941	4,476	3,247	3,766	—	—	—	—	63,524	60,427	—	—	1,749	1,509
Total ..	5,939	6,278	7,634	8,585	1	—	—	—	154,877	147,849	—	—	3,687	3,137

NOTE: Acute pneumonia ceased to be notifiable on 28 September 1968.

| | Smallpox | | Acute Encephalitis | | | | Enteric or typhoid fever | | Paratyphoid fever | | Tuberculosis (all forms) | | Acute meningitis | | Food poisoning | |
| | | | Infective | | Post-infectious | | | | | | | | | | | |
	M	F	M	F	M	F	M	F	M	F	M	F	M	F	M	F
Under 5 years	—	—	11	11	20	12	8	14	25	17	209	216	336	628	755	614
5–14 years	—	—	26	11	30	24	19	10	37	28	420	344	213	131	751	550
Total ..	—	—	37	22	50	36	27	24	62	45	629	560	549	399	1,506	1,164

APPENDIX C

STATISTICS OF THE SCHOOL DENTAL SERVICE

TABLE I

STAFF OF THE SCHOOL DENTAL SERVICE

	Dental* Officers		Dental* Auxiliaries		Dental Surgery Assistants		Dental* Hygienists		Dental Technicians		Dental Health Education Personnel		Clerical Assistants	
	1969	1970	1969	1970	1969	1970	1969	1970	1969	1970	1969	1970	1969	1970
Number:														
England	1,794	1,812	168	178	1,781	1,876	22	22	144	106	29	21	145	143
Wales ..	120	130	14	14	111	118	1	1	4	3	2	3	12	15
Total ..	1,914	1,942	182	192	1,892	1,994	23	23	148	109	31	24	157	158
Whole-time Equivalent:														
England	1,247·2	1,264·7	147·3	147·5	1,580·7	1,648·4	14·9	12·5	95·1	100·8	10·1	9·5	97·1	106·2
Wales ..	78·6	92·5	12·0	12·6	86·6	99·9	0·1	0·1	4·0	3·0	2·0	2·1	9·7	12·3
Total ..	1,325·8	1,357·2	159·3	160·1	1,667·3	1,748·3	15·0	12·6	99·1	103·8	12·1	11·6	106·8	118·5

* Excluding Maternity and Child Health.

TABLE II

Inspection and Treatment during the year ended 31 December

(A) Number of Pupils

Number of pupils on registers in January 1971 = 8,284,923 (England = 7,788,840 Wales = 496,083)

	First inspection			Number found to require treatment	Number offered treatment	Number actually treated	% age of pupils found to require treatment who received it	Number of pupils re-inspected at School or Clinic	Number of re-inspected pupils found to require treatment	Attendances made by pupils for treatment
	At school	At clinic	Total							
1969 England	3,615,315	631,291	4,246,606	2,367,020	2,062,094	1,233,825	52·12	412,227	245,499	3,283,473
Wales	155,384	45,405	200,789	130,217	119,065	78,630	60·38	19,100	12,884	190,485
Total	3,770,699	676,696	4,447,395	2,497,237	2,181,159	1,312,455	52·55	461,327	258,383	3,473,958
1970 England	3,694,769	669,990	4,364,759	2,419,679	2,114,935	1,230,585	50·85	435,555	258,737	3,347,194
Wales	163,725	49,042	212,767	137,665	127,803	83,693	60·79	20,219	13,061	216,217
Total	3,858,494	719,032	4,577,526	2,557,344	2,242,738	1,314,278	51·39	455,774	271,798	3,563,411

TABLE II—*continued*

(B) DENTAL TREATMENT (OTHER THAN ORTHODONTIC TREATMENT—SEE TABLE II(C))—DURING THE YEAR ENDED 31 DECEMBER

	Sessions devoted to			Number of fillings		Number of teeth filled		Number of extractions		Teeth otherwise conserved
	Treatment	Inspection	Dental health education	Permanent teeth	Deciduous teeth	Permanent teeth	Deciduous teeth	Permanent teeth	Deciduous teeth	
1969 England	524,355	34,935	16,238	1,967,407	842,098	1,671,279	749,265	261,766	819,297	162,453
Wales	34,821	2,107	1,366	114,556	40,527	93,085	35,915	21,884	62,029	15,161
Total	559,176	37,042	17,604	2,081,963	882,625	1,764,364	785,180	283,650	881,326	177,614
1970 England	531,574	33,259	14,723	2,044,650	905,216	1,725,941	806,891	262,264	797,599	155,640
Wales	37,124	1,958	1,015	124,937	50,363	100,340	43,363	22,605	63,245	14,612
Total	568,698	35,217	15,738	2,169,587	955,579	1,826,281	850,254	284,869	860,844	170,252

	Crowns	Inlays	Teeth root filled	Dentures		Number of pupils X-rayed	Prophylaxis	Number of general anaesthetics administered by	
				Number of pupils supplied with dentures	Number of dentures supplied			Dental Officers	Medical Practitioners
1969 England	5,447	838	6,539	5,807	7,093	87,933	323,991	103,822	238,392
Wales	332	35	530	502	542	3,526	17,503	6,114	26,459
Total	5,779	873	7,069	6,309	7,635	91,459	341,494	109,936	264,851
1970 England	6,030	799	7,340	5,571	6,833	95,616	349,333	92,729	233,966
Wales	338	36	559	496	531	4,081	21,250	6,514	25,173
Total	6,368	835	7,899	6,067	7,364	99,697	370,583	99,243	259,139

TABLE II—continued

(c) ORTHODONTIC TREATMENT DURING THE YEAR ENDED 31 DECEMBER

		Number of cases			Number of appliances fitted		Number of pupils referred to Hospital Consultants
		Commenced during the year	Completed during the year	Discontinued during the year	Removable	Fixed	
1969	England ..	22,225	15,895	3,637	36,145	2,126	4,646
	Wales ..	1,122	1,070	185	1,414	360	358
	Total ..	23,347	16,965	3,822	37,559	2,486	5,004
1970	England ..	21,603	17,931	3,564	36,874	2,235	4,300
	Wales ..	1,201	859	196	1,455	410	369
	Total ..	22,804	18,790	3,760	38,329	2,645	4,669

118

TABLE III

ATTENDANCE AND TREATMENT BY AGE GROUPS DURING THE YEAR ENDED 31 DECEMBER 1970

	Ages 5–9		Ages 10–14		Ages 15 and over		Total		Total England and Wales
	England	Wales	England	Wales	England	Wales	England	Wales	
Number of first visits (i.e. pupils treated)	628,816	44,071	503,782	32,703	97,987	6,919	1,230,585	83,693	1,314,278
Subsequent visits	862,805	57,701	1,035,511	60,949	218,293	13,874	2,116,609	132,524	2,249,133
Total visits	1,491,621	101,772	1,539,293	93,652	316,280	20,793	3,347,194	216,217	3,563,411
Additional courses of treatment commenced	77,123	3,122	62,960	2,353	12,181	584	152,264	6,059	158,323
Fillings in permanent teeth	545,141	31,971	1,185,565	71,848	313,944	21,118	2,044,650	124,937	2,169,587
Fillings in deciduous teeth	821,533	45,790	83,683	4,573	—	—	905,216	50,363	955,579
Permanent teeth filled	441,217	25,562	1,011,109	57,318	273,615	17,460	1,725,941	100,340	1,826,281
Deciduous teeth filled	732,088	39,311	74,803	4,052	—	—	806,891	43,363	850,254
Permanent teeth extracted	44,897	4,148	180,675	14,720	36,692	3,737	262,264	22,605	284,869
Deciduous teeth extracted	612,969	49,759	184,630	13,486	—	—	797,599	63,245	860,844
General anaesthetics	211,296	20,622	104,724	9,774	10,675	1,291	326,695	31,687	358,382
Emergencies (treatment)	89,678	8,217	48,674	3,106	9,287	689	147,639	12,012	159,651
Courses of treatment completed	—	—	—	—	—	—	1,111,867	63,151	1,175,018

TABLE IV

PROSTHETICS 1970 (BY AGE GROUPS)

		Ages 5–9	Ages 10–14	Ages 15 and over	Total
Pupils fitted with full denture for the first time	England ..	26	74	134	234
	Wales ..	1	4	19	24
	Total ..	27	78	153	258
Pupils supplied with other dentures for the first time	England ..	432	3,194	1,711	5,337
	Wales ..	29	241	202	472
	Total ..	461	3,435	1,913	5,809
Number of dentures supplied (first or subsequent time)	England ..	541	3,976	2,316	6,833
	Wales ..	31	256	244	531
	Total ..	572	4,232	2,560	7,364

TABLE V

ANALYSIS OF DUTIES OF DENTAL OFFICERS, DENTAL AUXILIARIES AND DENTAL HYGIENISTS FOR THE YEAR ENDED 31 DECEMBER ENGLAND AND WALES

i. Dental Officers

	Number of Officers		Total full-time equivalent inclusive of extra paid sessions worked					
			Administrative duties		Clinical duties			
					School Service		M & CH Service	
	1969	1970	1969	1970	1969	1970	1969	1970
PSDO	174	174	65·4	65·4	97·8	98·5	10·3	11·1
Dental Officers (employed on salary basis)	1,007	1,054	11·7	13·9	914·8	952·5	68·5	74·8
Dental Officers (employed on sessional basis)	733	714	—	—	235·8	226·9	17·5	18·5
Total	1,914	1,942	77·1	79·3	1,248.4	1,277·9	96·3	104·4

ii. Dental Auxiliaries and Dental Hygienists

	Number of Officers		Full-time equivalent			
			School Service		M & CH Service	
	1969	1970	1969	1970	1969	1970
Dental Auxiliaries	182	192	159·3	160·1	18·5	21·5
Dental Hygienists	23	23	15·0	12·6	1·4	4·0

APPENDIX D

HANDICAPPED PUPILS REQUIRING AND RECEIVING EDUCATION IN SPECIAL SCHOOLS APPROVED UNDER SECTION 9 (5) OF THE EDUCATION ACT, 1944: RECEIVING EDUCATION IN INDEPENDENT SCHOOLS, IN SPECIAL CLASSES AND UNITS; BOARDED IN HOMES AND RECEIVING EDUCATION IN ACCORDANCE WITH SECTION 56 OF THE EDUCATION ACT

		Blind	Partially sighted	Deaf	Partially hearing	Physically handicapped	Delicate	Mal-adjusted	E.S.N.	Epileptic	Suffering from speech defects	Total
1.	During the year ending 31st December, 1970, number of handicapped pupils who were:											
A.	Newly assessed as needing special educational treatment at special schools or in boarding homes	134	351	381	610	1836	2,251¹	3,428	12,392	253	135	21,771
B.	Newly placed in special schools (other than hospital special schools) or boarding homes	127	296	403	516	1,751	2,078	2,609	11,498	159	71	19,508
2.	In January 1971, number of handicapped children who were:											
A.	Requiring places in special schools (i) Day	5	76	56	131	425	254	242	8,235	6	30	9,460
	(ii) Boarding	86	142	65	73	316	425	1,623	1,879	47	63	4,719
B.	On the registers of maintained special schools (i) Day	21	1,232	1,552	1,036	6,350	4,246	2,243	47,677	171	128	64,656
	(ii) Boarding	220	393	541	392	1,217	1,931	2,337	7,888	101	35	15,055
C.	On the registers of non-maintained special schools (i) Day	30	33	206	63	286	1	5	306	—	3	933
	(ii) Boarding	847	422	1,271	494	1,199	695	981	1,186	472	90	7,657
D.	On the registers of independent schools under arrangements made by local education authorities	5	14	220	118	464	172	3,024	609	8	21	4,655
E.	Boarded in Homes and not already included in 2B, C or D above	1	—	4	—	11	112	685	18	3	—	834
F.	Being educated under arrangements made in accordance with Section 56 of the Education Act, 1944 (i) in hospitals	1	1	1	3	284	177	266	31	4	1	769
	(ii) in other groups	3	4	11	11	355	40	605	82	10	2	1,123
	(iii) at home	13	32	11	9	922	256	449	215	37	6	1,950
G.	Being educated in special classes or units not forming part of special schools	—	73	—	2,324	228	167	2,074	—	—	—	4,866
	Total receiving special educational treatment and awaiting places	1,232	2,422	3,938	4,654	12,057	8,476	14,534	68,126	859	379	116,677

(a) During 1970, 1,843 children were reported to Local Health Authorities as unsuitable for education under Section 57 (4) of the Education Act, 1944.
(b) In January 1971, 3,537 pupils were on the registers of hospital special schools but not included in the above table.

APPENDIX E

MEDICAL AND DENTAL STAFFS OF THE DEPARTMENT OF EDUCATION AND SCIENCE 1969/1970

Medical Officers

Chief Medical Officer*
Sir George Godber, K.C.B., D.M., F.R.C.P., D.P.H.

Senior Principal Medical Officers
Dr. P. Henderson, C.B., M.D., D.P.H. (Retired 20.9.69)
Dr. B. Didsbury, M.B., Ch.B., D.P.H. (From 22.9.69–3.9.70)

Principal Medical Officer
Dr. E. E. Simpson, M.D., B.S., F.R.C.P., D.P.H., D.C.H.

Senior Medical Officers
Dr. T. K. Whitmore, M.R.C.S., L.R.C.P., D.C.H.
Dr. M. Scott Stevenson, M.D., Ch.B., D.P.H.

Medical Officers
Dr. S. R. Fine, M.B., Ch.B., D.P.H., D.C.H., Barrister-at-Law
Dr. E. Wales, M.B., B.S., D.P.H., D.C.H., D.Obst.R.C.O.G.
Dr. M. W. Jenkins, B.Sc., M.B., B.Ch., D.P.H.†
Dr. N. P. Halliday, M.B., B.S., M.R.C.S., L.R.C.P., D.C.H.
Dr. M. B. Pepper, M.B., B.S., D.P.H.
Dr. R. Burns, L.R.C.P., L.R.C.S., L.R.F.P.S.
Dr. M. L. Graeme, V.R.D., M.A., M.B., B.Chir., M.R.C.S., L.R.C.P., D.P.H.

Dental Officers

Chief Dental Officer*
Surgeon Rear-Admiral (D.) W. Holgate, C.B., O.B.E., F.D.S., R.C.S.

Senior Dental Officer*
J. Rodgers, D.F.M., L.D.S., R.F.P.S.

Dental Officers
J. G. Potter, L.D.S., R.F.P.S.
W. G. Everett, L.D.S., R.C.S.
C. Howard, B.D.S., L.D.S., D.D.P.H., R.C.S.

*These officers are jointly employed by the Department of Health and Social Security and the Department of Education and Science

†This officer is jointly employed by the Welsh Office and the Department of Education and Science

SCHOOL HEALTH AND DENTAL SERVICES

TABLE SHOWING THE NAMES OF THE PRINCIPAL SCHOOL MEDICAL OFFICERS AND THE PRINCIPAL SCHOOL DENTAL OFFICERS EMPLOYED BY EACH LOCAL EDUCATION AUTHORITY, TOGETHER WITH THE NUMBER OF PUPILS ON THE REGISTERS OF MAINTAINED AND ASSISTED PRIMARY AND SECONDARY SCHOOLS (INCLUDING NURSERY AND SPECIAL SCHOOLS) IN JANUARY 1971.

ENGLAND (COUNTIES)

Local Education Authority	Name of Principal School Medical Officer	Name of Principal School Dental Officer	No. of Pupils on Registers January 1971
Bedfordshire	M. C. MacLeod	H. W. S. Sheasby	39,205
Berkshire	D. E. Cullington	G. Ogilvy	89,754
Buckinghamshire	J. J. A. Reid	C. H. Griffiths	105,196
Cambridgeshire and Isle of Ely	M. E. Hocken		46,728

123

Local Education Authority	Name of Principal School Medical Officer	Name of Principal School Dental Officer	No. of Pupils on Registers January 1971
Cheshire	B. G. Gretton-Watson	T. B. Dowell	190,378
Cornwall	H. Binysh	C. A. Reynolds	56,778
Cumberland	J. Leiper	R. B. Neal	40,334
Derbyshire	A. H. Snaith	H. E. Gray	112,735
Devon	J. Lyons	F. H. Stewart	62,637
Dorset	A. F. Turner	J. S. MacLachlan	54,698
Durham	S. Ludkin	Mrs. M. M. Lishman	152,380
Essex	J. A. C. Franklin	J. C. Timmis	206,743
Gloucestershire	A. Withnell	J. F. A. Smyth	97,099
Hampshire	I. A. MacDougall	C. C. Chadwick	172,167
Herefordshire	J. S. Cookson	O. S. Bennett	23,162
Hertfordshire	G. W. Knight	A. H. Millett	172,556
Huntingdon and Peterborough	G. Nisbet	I. O. Pinkham	37,891
Isle of Wight	R. K. Machell	G. Simons	15,679
Isles of Scilly	C. Mills	B. I. Fairest	280
Kent	A. Elliott	E. Millward	223,554
Lancashire	C. H. T. Wade	G. Entwisle	439,125
Leicestershire	A. R. Buchan	D. M. Hobbs	82,688
Lincolnshire Holland	J. Fielding	K. Jackson	17,535
Lincolnshire Kesteven	E. W. G. Birch	J. E. Mann	26,756
Lincolnshire Lindsey	C. D. Cormac	J. Watson	68,688
Norfolk	A. G. Scott	N. J. Rowland	68,504
Northamptonshire	W. J. McQuillan	P. W. Gibson	58,477
Northumberland	J. B. Tilley	A. E. Robinson	88,485
Nottinghamshire	H. I. Lockett	K. H. Davis	117,052
Oxfordshire	M. J. Pleydell	T. Lucas	45,922
Rutland	R. A. Matthews	Miss J. G. Campbell	4,680
Salop	P. C. Moore	C. D. Clarke	57,155
Somerset	A. Parry Jones	Q. A. Davies	92,787
Staffordshire	G. Ramage	W. McKay	129,732
Suffolk East	S. T. G. Gray	C. D. Macpherson	36,925
Suffolk West	D. A. McCracken	S. H. Pollard	26,108
Surrey	J. Drummond	O. H. Minton	149,491
Sussex East	J. A. G. Watson	C. K. Fenton Evans	57,242
Sussex West	T. McL. Galloway	P. S. R. Conron	74,158
Warwickshire	G. H. Taylor	H. J. Bastow	111,803
Westmorland	J. A. Guy	M. D. McGarry	11,410
Wiltshire	C. D. L. Lycett	D. Middleton	88,095
Worcestershire	J. D. Willins	C. W. D. Jones	71,663
Yorks, East Riding	W. Ferguson	G. R. Smith	41,195
Yorks, North Riding	J. T. A. George	Miss A. Potts	50,727
Yorks, West Riding	R. W. Elliott	H. Taylor	315,830

ENGLAND (COUNTY BOROUGHS)

Barnsley	G. A. W. Neill	G. White	14,437
Barrow-in-Furness	A. W. Hay	D. J. Harrison	11,401
Bath	R. M. Ross	G. G. Davis	12,534
Birkenhead	P. O. Nicholas	W. M. Shaw	24,509
Birmingham	E. L. M. Millar	F. J. Hastilow	190,552
Blackburn	J. Ardley	J. Rigby	18,078
Blackpool	D. W. Wauchob	M. Smith	20,455
Bolton	A. I. Ross	S. J. Bray	27,244
Bootle	G. T. MacCullock	D. N. Maxfield	16,126
Bournemouth	W. Fielding	Mrs. M. B. Redfern	18,473
Bradford	W. Turner	M. J. M. Mackay	56,526
Brighton	W. S. Parker	W. H. Garland	22,464
Bristol	R. C. Wofinden	J. McCaig	69,198
Burnley	L. J. Collins	C. F. Tehan	15,040

Local Education Authority	Name of Principal School Medical Officer	Name of Principal School Dental Officer	No. of Pupils on Registers January 1971
Burton-upon-Trent	R. Mitchell	A. N. Stannard	10,749
Bury	G. A. Levell	F. J. Heap	11,077
Canterbury	M. S. Harvey	B. J. West	5,969
Carlisle	D. G. Proudler	H. W. Freer	13,597
Chester	D. F. Morgan	G. H. Stout	11,493
Coventry	T. M. Clayton	J. A. Smith	63,496
Darlington	J. V. Walker	P. Waterfall	15,900
Derby	V. N. Leyshon	F. Grossman	38,084
Dewsbury	T. W. Robson	J. Tuxford	9,968
Doncaster	D. R. Martin	A. D. Anderson	16,382
Dudley	G. M. Reynolds	Mrs. J. P. McEwan	31,306
Eastbourne	K. O. A. Vickery	A. J. Lawrence	7,781
Exeter	G. P. McLauchlan	A. Pryor	13,948
Gateshead	D. F. Henley	Miss T. M. Rossi	16,486
Gloucester	P. T. Regester	R. Bell	18,122
Great Yarmouth	R. G. Newberry	B. C. Clay	9,037
Grimsby	R. Glenn	G. S. Watson	19,088
Halifax	J. G. Cairns	W. E. Crosland	16,687
Hartlepool	H. C. Milligan	Mrs. K. M. Atkinson	20,285
Hastings	T. H. Parkman	Mrs. E. M. Ward	9,733
Huddersfield	J. S. W. Brierley	J. A. E. Morris	23,117
Ipswich	B. A. Smith	G. A. Scivier	20,957
Kingston-upon-Hull	A. Hutchison	J. C. Carr	54,998
Leeds	D. B. Bradshaw	J. Miller	87,829
Leicester	B. J. L. Moss	R. H. Bettles	53,191
Lincoln	R. D. Haigh	G. A. Vega	13,821
Liverpool	A. B. Semple	P. E. Goward	120,091
Luton	R. M. Dykes	J. W. Coombs	31,400
Manchester	K. Campbell	G. L. Lindley	104,625
Newcastle-upon-Tyne	D. L. Wilson	J. C. Brown	37,253
Northampton	W. Edgar	P. W. J. L. Thompson	21,547
Norwich	J. R. Murdock	P. I. Christensen	19,484
Nottingham	F. E. James	N. H. Whitehouse	55,075
Oldham	B. Gilbert	J. Fenton	19,231
Oxford	J. F. Warin	C. H. I. Millar	17,361
Plymouth	T. A. I. Rees	T. S. Longworth	41,004
Portsmouth	P. G. Roads	P. D. Bristow	29,904
Preston	C. F. W. Fairfax	A. Kershaw	18,556
Reading	A. Gatherer	D. O. Mallam	23,064
Rochdale	R. G. Murray	H. W. Pritchard	17,104
Rotherham	I. F. Ralph	Miss J. H. Egan	16,238
St. Helens	J. H. E. Baines	J. P. H. Donovan	19,769
Salford	D. J. Roberts	E. Rose	25,802
Sheffield	C. H. Shaw	E. Copestake	88,596
Solihull	I. M. McLachlan	E. F. Stonehouse	19,273
Southampton	A. McGregor	A. J. Edwards	37,905
Southend-on-Sea	G. V. Griffin	J. M. Stratford	25,606
Southport	G. N. M. Wishart	W. L. Rothwell	13,007
South Shields	I. D. Leitch	T. W. Clarkson	18,710
Stockport	A. R. M. Moir	Miss F. Sellers	23,842
Stoke-on-Trent	J. S. Hamilton	G. T. Emery	47,214
Sunderland	A. Martin	F. J. Lishman	43,180
Teesside	R. J. Donaldson	R. C. Blackmore	86,061
Torbay	D. K. MacTaggart	G. J. Derbyshire	13,689
Tynemouth	G. MacA. Dowson	N. A. Eddy	13,629
Wakefield	D. B. Reynolds	R. E. Whittam	10,140
Wallasey	H. W. Hall	W. J. Meakin	17,415
Walsall	J. C. Talbot	Mrs. I. M. Millar	34,404
Warley	R. J. Dodds	J. Charlton	27,709
Warrington	E. H. Moore	A. C. Crawford	13,485

Local	Name of Principal School Medical Officer	Name of Principal School Dental Officer	No. of Pupils on Registers January 1971
West Bromwich ..	H. O. M. Bryant ..	J. B. C. Cuzner ..	30,907
Wigan	J. H. Hilditch ..	S. M. Aalen	14,064
Wolverhampton ..	F. N. Garratt.. ..	S. Awath-Behari ..	50,776
Worcester	G. M. O'Donnell ..	E. R. Dowland ..	13,296
York	S. R. W. Moore ..	G. Turner	18,677

LONDON

Authority	Name of Central Medical Adviser	Name of Central Dental Adviser	
Inner London	A. B. Stewart ..	K. C. B. Webster ..	

Authority	Name of Principal School Medical Officer	Name of Principal School Dental Officer	No. of Pupils on Registers January 1971
Inner London Boroughs			
Camden	W. G. Harding ..	G. P. Mailer	23,467
Greenwich	J. Kerr-Brown ..	F. Elston	40,260
Hackney	R. G. Davies	S. Gelbier	36,423
Hammersmith	A. D. Cameron ..	P. T. Fuller	26,749
Islington	C. Burns	R. E. Hyman	33,654
Royal Borough of Kensington & Chelsea	P. J. C. Walker ..		16,545
Lambeth	A. L. Thrower ..	B. M. Spalding ..	47,770
Lewisham	A. W. Tranter ..	Mrs. C. M. Leeming	45,368
Southwark	J. E. Epsom	J. J. Cleary	49,997
Tower Hamlets ..	R. W. Watton ..	D. F. Waller	31,660
Wandsworth	H. E. A. Carson ..	A. F. Weedon	49,033
City of Westminster ..	J. H. Briscoe-Smith ..	D. K. Hardy	22,405
City of London ..	W. G. Swann ..	L. J. Wallace	222
Outer London Boroughs			
Barking	J. A. Gillet	J. K. Whitelaw ..	28,161
Barnet	M. Watkins	R. L. James	44,942
Bexley	H. James	J. H. Forrester ..	35,328
Brent	E. Grundy	A. Henderson ..	42,622
Bromley	L. R. L. Edwards ..	Mrs. C. M. Lindsay ..	46,866
Croydon	S. L. Wright	J. D. Palmer	54,339
Ealing	I. H. Seppelt	L. C. Mandeville ..	45,180
Enfield	W. D. Hyde	T. J. H. Phillips ..	40,997
Haringey	J. L. Patton	G. C. H. Kramer ..	38,064
Harrow..	W. Cormack	A. G. Brown	30,389
Havering	F. Groarke	E. B. Hodgson ..	44,731
Hillingdon	J. S. Horner	Mrs. B. Fox	39,410
Hounslow	R. L. Lindon	D. H. Norman ..	32,093
Kingston-upon-Thames	J. C. Birchall	D. M. Dodd	20,060
Merton	P. J. Doody	M. T. Gibb	25,767
Newham	F. R. Dennison ..	P. A. Chandler ..	41,306
Redbridge	I. Gordon	E. V. Haigh	33,342
Richmond-upon-Thames	A. M. Nelson	G. H. Tucker	21,187
Sutton	W. H. Kinstrie ..	Mrs. B. M. Stewart ..	23,156
Waltham Forest ..	E. W. Wright	G. P. L. Taylor ..	34,196

WALES (COUNTIES)

Local Education Authority	Name of Principal School Medical Officer	Name of Principal School Dental Officer	No. of Pupils on Registers January 1971
Anglesey	G. Crompton	O. C. Jenkins	10,901
Breconshire	R. G. Evans	J. H. Sutcliffe	9,501
Caernarvonshire	C. T. Baynes	I. L. Williams	19,748
Cardiganshire	I. M. Watkin	W. D. P. Evans	9,352
Carmarthenshire	D. G. G. Jones	S. C. R. Evans	27,775
Denbighshire	M. T. I. Jones	D. R. Pearse	31,456
Flintshire	G. W. Roberts	A. Fielding	32,463
Glamorgan	W. E. Thomas	D. R. Edwards	135,847
Merioneth	E. Richards	E. C. Jones	6,084
Monmouthshire	A. J. Essex-Cater	E. F. Sumner	66,958
Montgomeryshire	E. S. Lovgreen	J. A. Reece	7,783
Pembrokeshire	D. J. Davies	D. G. James	18,680
Radnorshire	F. J. H. Crawford	P. G. H. Griffith	3,162

WALES (COUNTY BOROUGHS)

Local Education Authority	Name of Principal School Medical Officer	Name of Principal School Dental Officer	No. of Pupils on Registers January 1971
Cardiff	D. J. Anderson	H. V. Newcombe	52,526
Merthyr Tydfil	R. M. Williams	F. S. S. Baguley	10,235
Newport (Mon.)	W. Burns Clark	B. G. Hobby	22,562
Swansea	E. B. Meyrick	R. F. Hoar	31,050

Printed in England for Her Majesty's Stationery Office by McCorquodale Printers Ltd., London.
H.M. 5584.   Dd. 506050.   K 44.   10/72. McC. 3309

© Crown copyright 1972

SBN 11 270300 3

The Health of the

1972